You Are Psychic

THE ESSENTIAL
MIND BODY AND SPIRIT BOOKS

You Are Psychic

Intuition, skills, power

BelindaGrace

ROCKPOOL

A Rockpool book
PO Box 252
Summer Hill
NSW 2130
Australia

rockpoolpublishing.com
Follow us! **f** ⓞ rockpoolpublishing
Tag your images with #rockpoolpublishing

First published in 2007 as *You Are Clairvoyant* under ISBN: 9781921295041
Second edition published in 2017 under ISBN: 9781925429664

This edition published in 2026 by Rockpool Publishing
ISBN: 9781922468130

Copyright text © BelindaGrace 2026
Copyright design © Rockpool Publishing 2026

All rights reserved. No part of this publication may be reproduced,
stored in a retrieval system, or transmitted in any form or by any means, electronic,
mechanical, photocopying, recording or otherwise, without the prior written
permission of the publisher.

Design and typesetting by Sara Lindberg, Rockpool Publishing
First edition edited by Gabiann Marin

 A catalogue record for this
book is available from the
National Library of Australia

Printed and bound in China
10 9 8 7 6 5 4 3 2 1

Contents

Introduction	1
How to use this book	5
CHAPTER 1 ✦ How did I get here?	11
CHAPTER 2 ✦ The universe gives me my big break	19
CHAPTER 3 ✦ Why your imagination is your most important tool	25
CHAPTER 4 ✦ Getting more connected	35
CHAPTER 5 ✦ Meeting your Angels and Spirit Guides	59
CHAPTER 6 ✦ How to conduct a psychic conversation	79
CHAPTER 7 ✦ The art of automatic writing	93
CHAPTER 8 ✦ Writing letters to your Angels	107
CHAPTER 9 ✦ Breaking the cycle – releasing your past life patterns	119
CHAPTER 10 ✦ Parallel lives	139
CHAPTER 11 ✦ Healing self-sabotage – your personality aspects	149
CHAPTER 12 ✦ Creating heart and mind balance	167
CHAPTER 13 ✦ Do I have to meditate? – no, but it really does help!	179
CHAPTER 14 ✦ Our enlightened children	189
CHAPTER 15 ✦ Are you a star seed?	199
About the author	211
Acknowledgements	215

Introduction

Being psychic, intuitive or clairvoyant is not a magical skill selectively bestowed on some people. It is an innate ability that anyone can learn to develop. This powerful inner wisdom has been with you all along, just waiting to be switched back on again. Once you set your intention and commit to listening to your quiet, inner guidance rather than all the external noise, your abilities will begin to reactivate. There is no right or wrong way to experience your developing abilities, so use this book as a guide to help you gauge your own progress while embracing and learning from your own feelings and responses.

Rather than seeing psychic ability as a tool that will help you predict the future, it is much wiser and more powerful to understand the following: as you become accustomed to listening to your inner wisdom and knowing, and become comfortable with that sense of being divinely guided, you will instinctively and intuitively know what to do in the here and now. This is so much more important and powerful than focusing on a future scenario that may or may not happen.

What we create in our tomorrows stems from who and what we are today. So, being more connected to and willing to act on your psychic abilities and divine guidance in the present moment will make all the difference. If you truly do this, and let go of the immature desire to 'know the future', I can guarantee that this amazing and abundant Universe will deliver your dreams to you in magical ways that you could never have designed or controlled. This exciting life experience is then further enhanced by your willingness to truly tune in, because when opportunity knocks you will recognise and welcome it.

Our world has ever more distractions; everybody wants to sell you something or tell you how to think and feel. I honestly believe that there has never been a more important time in human history than NOW to trust in a wisdom that is beyond any kind of sales pitch. Learning to listen, trust and respond will bring you to a place of inner peace. A valuable experience that you can share with your family, friends and community.

Be prepared to start small, take baby steps and give yourself time to settle into this new way of being. Psychic development has no ultimate destination or agenda, so enjoy your unique journey and be open to the small daily miracles that abound.

BelindaGrace

Blessing, BelindaGrace

How to use this book

Clairvoyant or psychic intuition is no more difficult to learn than a new language or operating a computer program, but like anything 'new' to us, there is a learning curve, so it is necessary to apply yourself and practice. Nothing in this world is achieved without the will to make it happen. I like to call this your Intention.

Clairvoyance is an inner wisdom and connection that has been with you all along, just waiting to be switched back on again. If you have the intention then your clairvoyant abilities will be *reactivated*.

Each person has their own developmental pace. Sure, the Universe will give you plenty of nudges, but it never gives you more than you can handle, so your own psychic skills will open up at exactly the right time for you.

This book is designed to help you develop these skills through simple, effective exercises. Each technique is presented in a logical sequence and practicing each of the techniques will help you become more proficient with all the others.

There is no right or wrong way to experience your developing abilities. Use this book as a guide and my experiences as a reference to help you gauge your own progress, but embrace and learn from your own feelings, as you are the best judge of what feels right or otherwise for you.

I once met a very powerful psychic from America. She told me that in the first year of working with her newly developed awareness she allowed herself to get carried away with the supposed power of it all. She prayed and prayed to her God to let her see *everything*. One day she woke up and her whole world had changed; she could hear what people were thinking, she could see images around them of the memories of the pleasant and unpleasant things that they had done. She could see who was cheating on their partner, who was stealing money from their employer, who was feeling suicidal and all the other things that are often hidden behind our outer layers of civility.

This experience nearly sent her insane; and just as she had prayed for this ability, she beseeched her God to make it stop. She didn't want to know everything about everyone anymore. Once this deluge stopped she thanked her Angels and Spirit Guides for the abilities she had been given and resolved to be content with those. So be grateful for your small breakthroughs as they come and be patient; your intuitive development happens at a certain pace for a very good reason.

In the following pages you will hear a little about my own story and how I came to call myself a Clairvoyant Healer. This is a term or title that I love, but most people only focus on the 'clairvoyant' and miss the 'healer' part. The latter part is of course the most important, because what it means is that I am using the psychic skills that I have developed over the years to help people feel better. They come in confused and depressed and leave feeling uplifted and empowered in some way.

Predicting the future is not a big part of my practice. Occasionally the Angels will have something to say to a client about their future which is very precise, but generally they advise that there is no such thing as 'the future', there is no set plan or arrangement to depend upon. What they want us to understand is that there are numerous probable realities which can emerge, depending on the choices that you make and how happy you are within yourself in that moment.

What we create in our tomorrows stems from whom and what we are today, so being more aware and connected to your Divine Guidance in the present moment is very helpful. It is important to remember that as a psychic I am simply a Channel – for energy, *Light* and information. This book is not about my beliefs or opinions; it is about all the things that my Angels and Spirit Guides have taught me throughout my 20 years of practice. What you are about to read is what they have told me to 'do' and the information they have spoken through me numerous times in response to my own questions and those of my clients and students.

I am often amazed myself when I hear some of the things I am saying, because I know that they are not a direct product of my own knowledge, thought process or experience. In fact, they are the opposite, they are the product of not thinking, and just letting the information come through me.

My journey to where I am now has been a long one, with many twists and turns. In this book I aim to share with you some of the wonderful things that I have been taught along the way by my Spirit Guides, Angels and other non-physical friends; and perhaps enable you to see your way a little more clearly and avoid some of those detours that I encountered.

CHAPTER 1

How did I get here?

'I regularly receive readings from Belinda — I have not experienced anything quite like them! They provide me with information that brings me into a closer healing connection with myself, my Angels and my Spirit Guides . . . this has not only provided me with deep healing at the physical, emotional, mental and spiritual levels, it also always results in me feeling supported, guided and "on track" at the end of each session.'

J.L.

'Have you always been psychic?' 'When did you first realise you were psychic?' or 'How did you become a Clairvoyant Healer?'

These are the most common questions people ask me when they find out what I do for a 'living'. All very reasonable questions given that most people don't meet a psychic every day and it is an area shrouded in a bit of mystery. But the other reason, I believe, that people are so interested in the answers to these questions, is because everyone is naturally intuitive and clairvoyant, and it excites them to find out how they might develop these skills. They recognise something of themselves in me or what I do.

I often liken clairvoyance to an artistic skill. Anyone can paint, draw or learn a musical instrument if they really apply themselves. Even if you are musical or artistic by nature, you still have to take the time and make the effort to refine and develop your raw skills in a meaningful way. You want to be able to be creative and productive 'on demand', and becoming well practiced in your techniques will help you with that.

Being psychic is the same. It is an innate skill that we are all born with, there are no exceptions. Some people will have more of a flair for certain techniques than others, and some of you may have to practice more or persevere until you find the instrument or technique that works best for you. But with practice and a positive attitude your psychic and intuitive skills will reawaken in you once more.

When I was a child and a teenager growing up, any information about the so-called supernatural or metaphysical fascinated me. I occasionally had dreams that would show me, in a general or allegorical way, events that would then happen a few days later. I sometimes felt that I could see or hear 'ghosts', and I used to astral travel in my sleep so frequently and so clearly that I would sometimes wake with a jolt, feeling air-sick from the up and down motions I had been making in the skies.

One night when I was around 10 years old, I woke up to see my grandmother floating in the bedroom at the end of my bed. I saw her long, flowing grey hair and her nightdress, but I was not afraid, even though I knew she lived thousands of miles away in Switzerland! Having just awoken from a deep sleep, I blinked and looked again, but she was still there. She waved, but she seemed to be looking off somewhere into the distance and after waving for a while she simply drifted out through the wall.

The following morning a telephone call from Switzerland came to advise my mother that her mother had passed away.

Twenty years later another interesting event on my mother's farm prompted a discussion about 'spirits' and what happens to people after they die. It was then that I told my mum about what I had seen the night my grandmother had died. Mum was amazed because it had been reported to her that minutes before my grandmother drew her last breath, she had sat up in bed as best she could and waved to something or someone seemingly off in the distance.

By now you are probably thinking 'Well she was obviously born with this ability, I can't do this kind of thing'. But I never thought of myself as clairvoyant or as having some sort of gift. Take a few minutes to think back on your own childhood and you will probably find that you too had some interesting experiences or dreams that were usually explained away by your parents as being just your imagination.

Many of us had invisible friends and believed in ghosts or spirits, or just *knew* things in advance when we were children. These experiences are a result of our natural intuitive faculty, which sadly gets shut down in most children as they grow up, because we live in a world that does not know how to help us explore and expand on these natural gifts.

For me back then, these were seemingly random events and certainly didn't happen at my beck and call. They happened to me and I often could not predict or even make sense of them. As my teens turned into my 20s I became much more concerned with the 'real world' and most of these kinds of experiences became a thing of the past, with one notable exception.

In 1985 I was travelling in California with my boyfriend. We had very little money and decided to try hitch-hiking from Los Angeles to San Francisco to save on the cost of bus fare. We had intended to only accept rides that would take us along the coastal roads, but one very kind fellow said he would take us all the way to Santa Barbara if we didn't mind an inland diversion through the desert. We agreed, and settled back to enjoy our free and scenic ride.

After some time of driving up a long, gentle slope in the vast terrain, we came up and over the crest, revealing a large shallow valley spreading out before us for miles. My heart jumped, because even though I had never been there before physically in this lifetime, I recognised this place as somewhere I had flown over numerous times in my astral travels! It was an amazing experience to be there again, this time on the ground.

Once again, even though that experience excited and shook me up somewhat, there was nothing I could really 'do' with it, I just accepted it and moved on.

After graduating from high school and studying fashion design for three years, I headed out to travel the world. My intuitive connections had already shut down; ignored as I concentrated on the demands of everyday life. I remained in London for three years; enjoying the life of the consummate party girl and took to drinking, smoking, and the work hard/play hard lifestyle with gusto.

If anyone had said to me that I would be a psychic with a thriving practice one day I would have considered them crazy.

In London I worked as a sales rep for a great company in Convent Garden, full of young people, many from other countries just like me. The friends I made there are people who I treasure and stay in contact with to this day.

My life was all about business, money, travel and most of all, having fun. But as my social life flourished, my health deteriorated. What I didn't know then was that the deterioration of my health and the bucket loads of antibiotics prescribed to me by doctors would lead me to the place that I am at now.

As much as I loved England, the time came for me to return to Australia and the industry I was convinced I was cut out for: fashion.

I entered the fashion industry, rising through the ranks as state sales manager, national sales manager and finally landing a great job as a buyer for a national ladies wear chain. A good salary, a company car and business class overseas travel were all part of the job. I should have been happy, but the opposite was true, I was very depressed emotionally and my immune system, already weakened by my previous London lifestyle, became weaker. My bouts of chronic tonsillitis became worse and the medications stronger.

My health was spiralling downward at an alarming rate and I didn't know what to do; small doses of antibiotics became large, and still no real improvement was forthcoming.

My emotional health was also teetering. I can remember being so depressed in those last months in the fashion world that I could hardly get out of bed. Crying as I showered and dressed to go to work became the norm.

What I didn't understand then was that I was so out of harmony with my own truth that I was making myself miserable and ill. I thought there was something wrong with me at a psychological level. Then, as it always has, the Universe handed me a lifeline and, following my flatmate's advice, I went to see an alternative health practitioner who helped change the course of my life.

After nearly two years of homoeopathic remedies, herbal mixtures and kinesiology treatments I felt much better and was able to realise that the lifestyle and career path I had chosen weren't what I needed or really wanted. I announced that I wanted to change my life and do something in the alternative health field. My practitioner suggested that I study homoeopathy, which seemed to trigger a prophetic dream that very same night, and a certainty in me about this new direction.

Simply put, my dream was one of me standing on a beautiful beach at dawn. There was a lovely, old timber door floating out over the horizon, and as the sun came up, the door slowly opened, bathing me in the warm and glowing light. A beautiful dream to be sure, but it wasn't just the content of the dream that inspired me, it was the *feelings* I had during it and after I woke up. I felt so calm and happy and certain that I had been led to my new path.

Later that day I enrolled in a natural therapies college and I have never looked back.

Although I stopped practicing homoeopathy, that was what led me to work as a Clairvoyant Healer, as I met people who introduced me to other courses of study in the healing realm. Eventually I was accepted into a small class taught privately in a woman's home on Sydney's lower North Shore. There were about 10 of us in this group and we worked together for two years. Our teacher taught us the basics of Channelling, seeing auras or energy fields and how to feel and sense the chakras.

Finally the day came when I had graduated from college with my Diploma of Homoeopathy, and two years of studying the basics of spiritual healing under my belt. Oddly enough, I still saw myself as a homoeopath, believing that most people would not be interested in the chakra balancing work, let alone be prepared to pay for it.

After months of struggling with very few homoeopathy clients to help me pay my bills, I decided to let people know I could balance chakras. That was really all I could do. Sometimes I would receive a little information, and I could sense the chakras spinning and see their colours in my mind's eye, but that was it.

What amazed me was the interest that was aroused and the large number of clients who came in for what I regard now as a very simple treatment. My practice was in North Sydney, so most of my clients worked in the local corporate offices, some of them at very high levels. It often happened that if one of my clients was a CEO, GM or MD that he or she would instruct me not to phone their office because they didn't want other people at work to know that they were visiting someone like me. Despite all the hide and seek, most of my clients were extremely receptive and appreciative; proving this to me on a regular basis by recommending me to others (eventually!) and helping this area of my practice to take off.

CHAPTER 2

The universe gives me my big break

'Whenever I have a treatment with Belinda I feel so much lighter afterwards; it's like a physical, emotional and spiritual detox and realignment all in one. Sometimes I laugh or cry, and the information I receive and the lift I get are always great. I feel like I have taken important steps along my own path to wholeness and I feel more connected to the oneness that is Life.'

ROSEMARY

All of this was well and good and I was delighted to have clients and an increasingly stable source of income, but I was stubborn. I had just finished three years of homoeopathy study and was undertaking a fourth postgraduate year, while I built up my practice. Not recognising the clues that the Universe was giving me, I continued to believe that I was supposed to be a homoeopath and that the chakra balancing, which was the area of my practice which was really taking off, would simply remain a useful sideline.

I went to great lengths to market myself as a homoeopath and to convert my chakra balancing clients into homoeopathic clients as well. Mostly to no avail. Lost in my idea of 'the way things should be', and needing a stronger hint, the Universe obviously decided that it needed to give me a kick in the backside – metaphorically speaking of course!

I received the Cosmic Boot while balancing the chakras of a new female client. This young woman was no more than 25, but there was something a little disturbing or dark about her energy, despite her friendly and open personality.

As I worked upon one of her chakras it was as though someone suddenly switched on a large, full colour screen inside my mind. I could see terrible scenes of soldiers beating and even shooting unarmed civilians. They looked like peasants being persecuted by armed forces and I had the immediate feeling that it was somewhere in South America. Not knowing what to do, I watched for a few seconds in utter amazement. I wondered 'What is going on here?' and I heard a voice inside my mind explain: 'It's her past life, tell her about it.'

I have no idea how well I did that day. I did my best to describe everything to her that I could see, hear and feel; this same voice speaking through me to fill in a lot more of the detail.

My client was intrigued and felt that she could relate to much of what had come through in the 'story'. She had no idea that this was the first time I had experienced this kind of information download, and while she left feeling 'lighter' than when she had come in, I was left to ponder the meaning of what had just occurred.

As days turned to weeks, and my practice continued to expand, the downloading of these movies and the commentary that accompanied them became clearer and more detailed.

For a while I still wrestled with my belief that I was destined to be a homoeopath, realising only much later that homoeopathy, and that all-important diploma, was the path by which I was meant to arrive at this place.

I have an enormous respect for homoeopathy and the dedicated practitioners who work with it. The four years of study gave me a foundation and a confidence in dealing with clients that I would never have had if I had studied Clairvoyant Healing alone. To this day I still visit my own homoeopath here in Sydney for a chat and a remedy, and derive much benefit from it, but it was not meant to be my actual career, it was the thing that prepared me for what was.

As for my interesting 'sideline', well, it completely took over my practice and I finally learned to let go a bit and do what I was told!

Now, I know what you are thinking, no matter how hard you tried, this sort of thing would never happen to you, but the truth is it could and does happen to any number of people, and even more so if you are open and receptive to it. Undertaking the techniques in this book is, in part, your message to the Universe that you are ready and willing to listen to whatever it needs to tell you.

Remember it took me a while to really listen too, but after that initial experience I decided to trust what I was being told and shown; and that is the most important requirement of all when it comes to developing clairvoyant abilities. Instead of negating these experiences I realised that all of this information was coming to me because the client on the table needed to know about it. So, instead of getting in the way, I decided I would be the clearest Channel for this information that I could be.

The only confirmation that has ever mattered to me is the feedback from the clients themselves. If they had looked at me like I was crazy and told me I was talking a load of rubbish, then the only sensible thing to do would have been to stop. Instead, I found time and again that my clients related so much to what came through me that they often cried, usually hugged me, came back for more and sent their family and friends in as well.

Since those humble beginnings I have also developed courses through which I am able to teach and share what I do with small groups of students. It always amazes and delights me when I see how quickly they blossom with things that took me years to learn. Within weeks, many of my students are reading past life information, communicating with Angels and balancing chakras in a natural and confident way. They are the living proof that you can do this work too if you are simply willing to try.

The techniques that you are going to learn and use from this book will help you to be as clairvoyant as you wish to be in your life, but only if you practice them. I didn't just wake up one day and feel: 'Wow, I'm clairvoyant!' I worked at it for years in class and on clients to hone my skills.

Every time I received instructions or guidance to do something that was new to me I followed it without question, because I always felt safe, protected and loved while I did this work and my clients always gave me positive feedback.

Every technique that is described in this book has been taught to me by my Angels and Spirit Guides – my teachers – for the last 10 years, and are the same techniques that I teach in my classes.

You will learn how to meet your own celestial friends and how to develop your psychic and channelling skills in various ways. Like me, you should let your feelings be your guide, and if you are more comfortable using some techniques than others, then you should persevere with them.

Not everybody wants to do what I do as a profession, but we can all use more information, guidance and clarity when it comes to navigating the journey of life. The techniques you will learn from this book will help you to become more connected to a higher source of guidance and awareness than that available if you only rely on your intellectual knowledge or logical mind.

Many people come to see me because they feel stuck, uninspired, lost or depressed. They have lost contact with the meaning and purpose of their lives. So these are the tools we give to them in order to help them bring the meaning and purpose back.

There are many different and valid ways to approach and make the most of your life's journey. This book does not claim to hold all the cures for personal and societal ills. It is a starting point, and I believe a very important one, because it demystifies something that all of us have; a profound and natural intuitive and clairvoyant capacity. I trust that you will enjoy uncovering, rediscovering and developing your own.

CHAPTER 3

Why your imagination is your most important tool

'From this moment on I choose to honour the creative power and principal that is natural in me. The Divine Gift of my imagination will help me now and evermore in my quest to better understand and love myself, and all that is.'

AFFIRMATION FOR IMAGINATION

The imagination is your interface and interpreter. It is the bridge between the physical and the non-physical worlds. If you let it open up new worlds and understanding for you, it will prove to be a great gift.

How many times have you heard someone say: 'Oh, it's just your imagination', or 'I was probably just imagining it.'

Statements like these can sometimes imply that the imagination is a second rate or unreliable function of our minds. Because for many people the imagination is not 'real'; it is considered to be something untrustworthy or even worse, something to be feared.

These days many people look to science as the only reliable measure of what is true and real in our world, yet the same scientists who develop their tests, theories and concepts are using their imagination to do so. You could say that our imagination is the first step in the creation of anything, whether it is building a computer, designing an item of clothing or creating a work of art. Before any item can be created in the physical realm it has to start as an idea, so where would the human race be without imagination?

In the same way that our imagination helps us bring something to life, it also helps us to connect with the levels of life that we cannot perceive with our five physical senses. There is so much more going on around us than what our eyes can see or our ears can hear.

For instance a dog can hear sounds of a much higher pitch than our human ears can, and certain types of tropical fish can see colours outside of the spectrum that we consider to be normal. Electricity is

WHY YOUR IMAGINATION IS YOUR MOST IMPORTANT TOOL

not visible, yet much of our world runs on it, and waves of different frequencies create for us the very real experiences of listening to the radio or watching television.

Just like a television or a radio needs an aerial or an antenna to receive this information, and the wiring within to translate it into sound or pictures for us, so too do we humans have ways of collecting and translating information from the Universe for ourselves. I call these The Channel and The Inner Screen.

In the next chapter I will describe to you how to re-activate those parts of your spiritual anatomy so that your own antenna will be able to start receiving again. But for now I would just like you to contemplate the idea that your imagination is the interpreter that takes in all this newly received data and helps you to decipher it.

The music on your radio and the pictures on your television screen are transmitted in one format and then translated into another so that your senses can comprehend it. When your Channel receives information from your Divine Guidance, Guardian Angel, the Universe or whatever you would like to call it, your imagination then converts those frequencies into feelings, thoughts, words or images that you can understand.

Your imagination is the *bridge*, the vital link we all have, between our physical and non-physical worlds.

In order to exercise and strengthen your imagination, and help your vital link to function, there are some simple exercises you can do. You won't need to set aside much time to do these exercises either, as you can do them while performing simple tasks like going for a walk or riding to and from work. There is nothing difficult about developing what is already one of your natural assets. It is meant to be easy, interesting and fun. The most important ingredient is your intention, and if you intend to let the words in this book and the Universe guide you, then you will experience some wonderful results.

EXERCISE ONE

EXERCISING YOUR IMAGINATION

When someone says they can't visualise things very well, especially something that is not normally seen, like an Angel, I ask them to imagine something more common to their everyday experience. This exercise is designed to help you get used to using your imagination.

REQUIREMENTS: a quiet space where you can sit or lie comfortably

TIME REQUIRED: a few minutes

- Close your eyes and sit quietly for a minute or two and allow yourself to visualise a red sports car with lovely, shiny chrome wheels, a roof that comes down and white stripes along its sides. You will be able to imagine it even if you have never seen a car exactly like this before.

- Use your own imagination to fill in the gaps, you create it yourself, which is the whole point of using your imagination in the first place. Your red sports car will be unique to your own imagination, because you have put your own original spin on it.

- By doing this exercise you are re-activating your Inner Screen, the mind's eye which interprets information and guidance into visual pictures.

VARIATION

Another way you can exercise your Inner Screen is by deciding what clothes you want to wear at a future point in time.

- Close your eyes and imagine what you may wear to work tomorrow, or picture an outfit you could wear to a party on the weekend.

- In your mind go through your wardrobe and imagine yourself in this or that outfit until one feels right.

- Hold these images for a few moments then let them fade.

- Repeat this simple exercise for a few moments each day.

This is your imagination in action and gives you a good example of what psychic sight feels like. It is not like seeing a solid object with the naked eye, but it is just as clear and real.

Once you become accustomed to this practice you can challenge yourself by trying to imagine an Angel, allowing your imagination to create an Angel which is unique to you.

EXERCISE TWO

IMAGINING AN ANGEL

REQUIREMENTS: a quiet space where
you can sit or lie comfortably

TIME REQUIRED: a few minutes

- Close your eyes and sit quietly for a few moments and give yourself permission to imagine an Angel.

- Imagine this Angel however you would like them to be. It won't matter if you have never 'seen' an Angel before as you can determine exactly what your Angel looks like.

- Maybe your Angel will look like the traditional representation with big golden wings and a halo, or like a small cherub or even a ball of pure silver light. However your Angel appears to you is fine; there is no right way or wrong way to imagine an Angel.

- Let the image play gently in your mind. Do not try to grab onto any particular image. Welcome them all as they come and allow them gently to fade away.

- Take pleasure in this simple exercise and let it be fun. Repeat it for a few minutes whenever you like.

WHY YOUR IMAGINATION IS YOUR MOST IMPORTANT TOOL

Your imagination is a very valuable tool. Use it, exercise it, treasure and respect it because it is your vital link to the beauty and magic of all the non-physical levels of your life. The suppression of our truly creative and original imagination is one of the great tragedies of human life.

When someone has a great idea or a child shows artistic talent, it is often disregarded because it has no monetary value. Using your imagination is not the same as being impractical or trying to escape reality, it is one of the tools given to us so that we may expand and evolve as human and spiritual beings; it is the birthplace of all the things we consider to be real.

Now we come to the most important point about your imagination, this wonderful tool that we all have that needs to be nurtured and cherished. Your imagination is the *bridge* between this physical reality and all the other realities you long to connect with.

Imagination is synonymous with inspiration, it is the link between the Divine Guidance that we all need and the thinking mind that can decide to act upon it. It literally bridges the gap between what is tangible to our senses as human beings and that which is available to us in unlimited quantity as spiritual beings. You will never be truly intuitive or psychic if you do not engage your imagination.

Your Divine Guidance will bring you support and inspiration in a way that is uniquely tailored to your understanding, and your imagination will help to translate it into a form that your mind can relate to and work with. No two people will ever imagine something in exactly the same way.

Spirit Guides can appear to us in unlimited ways. Your Spirit Guides and Angels will look different to anyone else's even when it is an Angel that everyone knows about, such as one of the Archangels. They are not restricted to a physical form and can change their appearance at will.

The human obsession with nailing everything down and saying that this is the right way so everything else must be wrong is very destructive indeed. In many peoples' eyes you would still be deemed wrong to imagine an Angel to be anything other than a brightly lit being with wings. But you wouldn't be wrong because you cannot put limitations on something that is truly without limits.

Use the affirmation for imagination which heads this chapter whenever you need to feel proud of your imagination and your ability to use it constructively in your life. It is a gift that all of us have and all of us need to nurture, in order to benefit ourselves, and the wider world we touch every day.

CHAPTER 4

Getting more connected

'Belinda, thank you so much for an incredible healing session. It was truly transformational. I have now put things into proper perspective and am dealing with my issues proactively. I no longer feel pulled in two directions as there is only one road to travel.'

STEVE L.

Remember back in chapter two when the Universe gave me a shove in order to help me see some past life information for my client? Well it was the daily tune ups that I gave my own chakras, Channel and Inner Screen that enabled me to receive all that detailed information. Six months prior to that breakthrough I wasn't seeing or hearing much at the psychic level. Almost every day I did one of the exercises that I am going to describe for you shortly and slowly but surely my connection improved.

I again noticed this improved connection when a lady in her mid 50s came to see me. As soon as I put my hands on her navel chakra I kept hearing the word 'hysterectomy' repeated over and over again. Finally I worked up the courage to ask her if she had had such an operation.

At first she looked a bit startled but soon opened up about what an awful experience it had been, how there had been complications during and after the operation, infection and continuing soreness in the scar tissue. Her emotional response as well as physical discomfort from the procedure was still very strong even though the operation had been 15 years earlier.

I went with my feelings and spent most of the treatment time sending the healing light and energy into that part of her body. Months later she sent me a card to let me know that the discomfort in that area of her body had diminished a great deal after that session, and her hormone balance and moods improved. If I had not been open to receiving this information she would not have had the benefits from this chakra clearing.

Many interesting experiences like this continued to happen, and the more I worked on strengthening and clearing my own spiritual anatomy, the more detailed the information became. Since the day of my 'big breakthrough' the expansion hasn't stopped. I continue to do what I call my Spiritual Maintenance and the Universe keeps teaching me more new and wonderful techniques.

The term 'Use it or lose it' doesn't just apply to your physical and mental fitness, it applies to your intuitive fitness as well. Remember, this is just the beginning of your journey – it all gets better from here.

Think of it this way, if there is a tap in your home that you haven't used for years and you turn it to let the water begin to flow again you won't get clear, clean water at first. The pipes might have become rusty; there will be air bubbles and other obstructions. The water will sputter and spurt and be grubby.

Do you give up on it, turn it off and walk away? No of course not! You let the water run for a while and use it regularly until it comes back to normal; the very act of using it is the repair and maintenance that it required. So it is with your spiritual anatomy. You will be a bit rusty at first, but there is no reason to be disheartened. By doing the following exercises regularly you will get your 'water' flowing again, no problem.

Your chakras, Channel and Inner Screen are the three most important 'tools' that you will work with from now on. As a budding psychic you will learn that keeping your chakras healthy and strong is vital. Very soon I will give you some techniques for activating your Channel and Inner Screen, but first, let's have a look at some basic knowledge about the chakras so you can understand why they are so important and get you motivated to give them regular care.

Chakras – a beginner's guide

There are thousands of books about chakras, their history, purpose and function, but at this stage you only need to know the nutshell version. Some of you may already know more than what is written here, and if that is the case feel free to skip onto the exercise.

The word 'chakra' comes from the ancient language of Sanskrit and means 'wheel of light'. The chakras are major energy centres within us that support all the functions of our physical and spiritual bodies. Buddhist and Hindu texts have been referring to the importance of balanced and healthy chakras for around 5000 years.

Having a basic understanding of the chakras and their purpose is very helpful in many areas of life. They greatly affect your physical, emotional and spiritual health. We all know how our blood circulates around the body, delivering life-giving oxygen and nutrients to every tissue and cell. We have also come to understand that our circulation aids in the removal of unwanted, toxic or spent materials from our bodies. When circulation of blood is poor, it can affect our health in many different ways.

The chakras and the many channels of energy that connect them, known as *nadis*, work in a very similar way. There are seven main chakras in your body, located individually at the base of your spine, just below your navel, at your solar plexus, at the centre of your chest, over your throat, on your forehead above the bridge of your nose and on the top, or crown of your head.

There are also chakras on the soles of your feet, in or over every joint in your body and placed all around you in your aura or energy field. Some ancient Indian texts detail the existence of as many as 88,000 chakras. All of these chakras are then connected to each other through the network of *nadis* to form a vast circulation system for the Universal energy. Not the kind of energy that you think of in terms of calories or physical energy, but that beautiful, subtle and vital energy normally referred to as prana, qi or chi.

To an intuitive or psychic the chakras appear like spheres, circles or cones of spinning, coloured light. Often when I am working with one of my clients their chakras will display these characteristics along with many other forms. Frequently I will see their chakras as flowers, sometimes large and flat like gerberas, sometimes like a rose and at other times like the classic lotus flower as described in many ancient spiritual texts.

In a healthy state, the chakras will spin evenly and quickly and each one will glow brightly with the particular colour of the light spectrum at which they vibrate. Altogether the seven main chakras make up the colours of the rainbow.

A weak, tired or stressed chakra can feel very sluggish or have a very unbalanced, elliptical spin. On your Inner Screen you might see the chakra as being dull or dark, rather than the lovely bright colour it should ideally be.

All chakras have very special functions and none is more important than another. In time, as you learn more about them you will realise that they all have a vital role to play. For the purposes of developing your intuition the brow chakra, or third eye, is the one that most people have heard about and we will be discussing its function in more detail later.

Put simply, the chakra system draws in energy or life force from the Universe and distributes it throughout your body and energy field. They also give out energy and are significant in composing the 'vibe' that each of us feel from other people and emanate from ourselves.

Have you ever wondered how it is that you can sense another person's happiness or anger without even speaking to them, or why it is that you are drawn to certain people and not to others? The condition and activity of each person's chakra system creates a flow of energy around them that is unique, and while the quality of this energy can fluctuate a great deal depending on mood, health, circumstances and so on, it will always reflect the total composition of that person at any given moment.

Each chakra has a special significance and function and corresponds to certain areas of your physical body, emotions and stages of life. Here is a basic guide to the seven main chakras.

THE CROWN CHAKRA

The 1000 petal lotus, located on the top of your head.

COLOUR: Violet, gold, white.
BODY/MIND CONNECTION: The brain.
ELEMENT: All.
SENSES: That which is beyond our senses.

Represents the connection to our purest form of being. A healthy crown chakra takes you towards pure consciousness and unity with the Universal energy. It is the chakra of enlightenment.

THE BROW CHAKRA OR THIRD EYE

The 96 petal lotus, located on the forehead just above the bridge of the nose, extending from the front to the back of the head.

COLOUR: Indigo, magenta.
BODY/MIND CONNECTION: Face, eyes, ears, sinuses, pituitary gland.
ELEMENT: All.
SENSES: All, including intuition and clairvoyance.

Represents knowledge and awareness of being. Takes you beyond an active mind and intellect, to a deeper understanding of Universal truths. Increases your capacity for visualisation, trust in your intuition and an ability to see beyond the surface meanings of life. Functions as your all-important Inner Screen, acting as a portal for all that you will see. It is the chakra of the Divine Wisdom that is available to all of us, beyond the conscious mind.

Meditating on your brow chakra and on the creation of your Inner Screen will reactivate and strengthen it. Fluorite is one of the many crystals that is said to increase the powers of your brow chakra and second sight.

THE THROAT CHAKRA

The 16 petal lotus, located over the throat, extending from the front to the back of the neck.

COLOUR: Sky blue, bright blue.
BODY/MIND CONNECTION: Voice, throat, jaw, neck, arms and verbal expression.
ELEMENT: Ether.
SENSES: Hearing.

Represents the way you express yourself. A healthy throat chakra improves self expression so that you may be truthful and clear. Also aids knowing when to be silent and listen to others or your own inner voice. It is the chakra of communication.

THE HEART CHAKRA

The 12 petal lotus, located over the lower sternum in the centre of the chest and extending through the chest to the back, between the shoulder blades.

COLOUR: Emerald green, pink.
BODY/MIND CONNECTION: Arms, heart, chest, lungs, skin, thymus gland, circulation.
ELEMENT: Air.
SENSES: Touch.

Represents the ability to give and receive love, freely and unconditionally. When healthy, it enables you to feel compassion for yourself and others, and experience the pure joy of living. It is the chakra of feeling empathy with all other living beings.

THE SOLAR PLEXUS CHAKRA

The 10 petal lotus, located on the centre of the midriff, extending to the back.

COLOUR: Golden yellow.
BODY/MIND CONNECTION: Stomach, digestion, nervous system, gut feel, instinct.
ELEMENT: Fire.
SENSES: Sight.

Represents the way in which you present yourself to the world. Brings a balanced attitude to the spiritual and material needs in your life and promotes acceptance of self. It is the 'I am' chakra and is connected to your development as an individual.

THE NAVEL CHAKRA

The 6 petal lotus, located on the lower abdomen, just below the navel and extending to the small of the back.

COLOUR: Orange.
BODY/MIND CONNECTION: Reproductive organs, kidneys, bladder, lymph, body fluids.
ELEMENT: Water.
SENSES: Taste.

Represents fundamental creativity of and in life. Allows you to be open to the flow of energy between male and female, enhances a balanced approach to sex, nurturing, emotions and intimacy. It is the chakra of family, relationships and belonging.

THE BASE CHAKRA

The 4 petal lotus, located at the base of the spine, between the legs.

COLOUR: Rich, crimson red.
BODY/MIND CONNECTION: Bones, teeth, nails, blood, muscle, the building of cells.
ELEMENT: Earth.
SENSES: Smell.

Represents your will to live and survival instincts. Connection to Mother Earth and Nature. A healthy base chakra keeps you in tune with the natural cycles of life, helps you to thrive and prosper, and keeps you centred and grounded. It is the chakra of human, physical form and embracing physical life as part of the human 'tribe'.

Once you have an understanding of how the chakras work, it is important to give them a little tune up from time to time. Daily is ideal, especially if you are exposed to a lot of people or negativity on a daily basis.

A few minutes a day taking care of your chakras will help to keep them and you feeling good, and will definitely make it easier for you to develop your intuition and psychic abilities. So let's get to it.

My Angels taught me that the simplest way to keep your chakras strong, clear and healthy is to purify them with Light. You can use white light or a rainbow, whichever you prefer. The chakras resonate to the colours of the rainbow, that is red, orange, yellow, green, blue, indigo and violet. White light contains all of these colours, so imagining a beam of white light flowing through your body, or a rainbow, will do the same job. Each chakra will absorb the colour that it needs from this spectrum to help strengthen and clear it.

EXERCISE THREE

CHAKRA CLEARING AND BALANCING

REQUIREMENTS: a quiet place where you can sit or lie comfortably

TIME REQUIRED: 2–15 minutes per day

- Start by sitting or lying down comfortably and closing your eyes.

- Imagine a beautiful beam of white light or rainbow light flowing down from the heavens and into the top of your head. Picture it streaming down in a strong, continuous flow, moving down through the centre of your body to the base of your spine. Just imagine the rich, healing Light flowing through and nurturing all of the seven main chakras.

- Along the way this Light will travel through each of these chakras, entering at the crown chakra on the top of your head and finishing at the base chakra at the base of your spine.

- Breathe deeply and relax so you enjoy this process, it takes very little effort and is really more a matter of just allowing it to happen rather than 'doing' it.

- Slowly open your eyes and enjoy the feeling of the energy flowing through your chakras and body as you bring yourself back to the room, re-orientating yourself with your surroundings.

Don't get stressed if you can't see the beam of light, it's nice to be able to, but not necessary in order for the process to work. Your intention is the most important ingredient in all of these processes, so as long as your general intention is to let the Light flow to you and through you in order to strengthen, balance and cleanse your chakras, then that is exactly what will happen.

How long and how often you give yourself this little treat is up to you. Spoil yourself and do it every day if you can! Between 2 and 15 minutes a day is plenty. You can do it when you wake up as a refreshing way to start your day, before you go to sleep at night to help you relax, or if you commute to work on public transport then go ahead and do it on the train, ferry or bus. It doesn't need to be any more complicated than that.

Your channel and how to activate it

Once you have cleared your chakras it is time to concentrate on your Channel.

Now, if your chakras are the luminous flowers or energy centres of your bodies' spiritual anatomy, then your Channel is like the great stem or trunk from which the seven main chakras grow. I sometimes like to refer to the Channel as your antenna because it is the instrument that you will activate and use in the receiving of all your Divine Guidance, whether it comes in words, sounds, pictures or as feelings.

Your Channel is already active to a certain degree, because just like the chakras, your Channel plays a vital role in the distribution of the life force energies in and around your body. In a sense the Channel is the major *nadi*, equivalent to the largest of our arteries. It is also known as the *sushumna*, but the word Channel is widely understood and will certainly suffice here.

A healthy Channel has the appearance of a strong and colourful beam or tube of light that shines down into your crown chakra and then travels through the core of your body to the base chakra. From the base chakra, or base of your spine, it then travels down both of your legs, out through the soles of your feet and deep into the core of the Earth. In this way your Channel connects you to the nurturing source of energy that is our physical home in this life, our dazzlingly beautiful planet. It also connects you to the highest possible level of your Divine Guidance, shining down into your crown and other chakras from the infinite realms of the Universe. Via your Channel, you become the connection point or junction between Heaven and Earth, a living, breathing receiver ready to bring Light and enlightenment into your world.

A beam of light coming to you from the Cosmos, shining in through the top of your head and down through the core of your body, sounds familiar doesn't it? You just achieved it in Exercise

Three, so you see, the benefits of that exercise are twofold because it will actually help you to clear and strengthen your Channel as well. You use your Channel to bring the Light down to your chakras and in so doing you also create a more powerful and receptive Channel, multitasking already, aren't you clever? And you thought this was going to be difficult.

Most peoples' Channels are weak and clogged at first; cluttered up with worry, fatigue, unresolved emotions and negative ideas or thoughts. Like the chakras, the Channel is not a solid, physical organ like your heart or lungs, but its healthy function is every bit as important.

Many times I have treated a client for a Channel that was damaged or unwell in some way and they have reported back to me their great feeling of relief and improved sense of wellbeing long after the healing was done. All manner of ailments including depression, lack of confidence, nausea, dizziness and other physical complaints can be improved or relieved by clearing your Channel and keeping it strong.

As your Channel becomes healthier you begin to notice other benefits, one of which is *you automatically become more intuitive*. Your Channel is now more open and free to bring you the information and guidance you desire.

For me, my Channel is an invaluable tool, the conduit for all my inspiration and the information I bring through for my clients. Here are some simple tips on how to clear and strengthen your own beautiful Channel.

EXERCISE FOUR

REACTIVATING YOUR FULL CHANNEL

REQUIREMENTS: a quiet location where you can sit or lie comfortably

TIME REQUIRED: 10–20 minutes

- Settle yourself comfortably and relax. Close your eyes when you are ready to begin.

- Imagine a beam of white light travelling down to you from way up in the Cosmos. Picture it travelling through the galaxies and into our solar system and making a beeline for you here on planet Earth.

- Let the white light shine onto the top of your head and down through your head and neck, and then through the length of your body. This beam of light will be cylindrical in shape, like a pipe or a tube and will flow through the centre of your body in front of your spine.

- Once it reaches your base chakra let it branch out and continue to flow down through both your hips and legs, passing through the upper legs, knees, lower legs and ankles to the soles of your feet.

- From there, picture the white light reforming into one branch again and flowing down through the floor and into the Earth, all the way to her core. Connecting your Channel to the Earth's core is very important because it helps to keep you grounded; being psychic is not about being 'off with the faeries' it is about bringing your Divine Guidance into your everyday, physical life.

GETTING MORE CONNECTED

- Sit for a moment and allow yourself to become reacquainted with the feeling of an active, connected and energised Channel.

- Now you have the Universal white light flowing through you from top to bottom, connecting, through you, from the Cosmos to the core of the Earth. The next step gives you an even stronger connection to the Earth's nurturing energy.

Note: Mother Earth is a soul and spirit in her own right and, as indigenous cultures have known for millennia, she is also the source of great wisdom. By tapping into her we tap into a level of our own wisdom which is generally overlooked by western society.

- From the core of the Earth, imagine a beautiful, rich red light, the colour of a fine red wine, travelling back up towards you. While the white light from above is vibrant and energising, the red light from the Earth is warm, comforting and nurturing.

- Feel it flow up through the soles of your feet and moving all the way back up through your Channel – legs, hips, core of your body and head – until it flows up and out through your crown chakra and into the Cosmos.

- Keep breathing deeply and steadily, giving yourself a few moments to become reacquainted with this flow of energy.

- Now you have the white light flowing down through your Channel and the warm, red light flowing up. These two energies will flow simultaneously without getting in each others' way.

- After a few minutes slowly open your eyes and reacquaint yourself with your surroundings. Your Channel will continue to be open and flowing.

- Repeat this exercise whenever you feel mentally or emotionally weakened or blocked; or any time you wish to strengthen your Channel.

What you have now is a fully functioning Channel that is probably more receptive than it's been since the earliest days of your childhood. Don't be dismayed if you didn't 'see' or feel much on your first attempt, it will come with practice.

Working with our intuition is about learning to relax and let it happen, rather than making it happen. Your sensitivity will increase with practice.

It is possible to have all kinds of mild reactions to the reawakening and clearing of your intuitive anatomy. Mild itching, tingling, or the desire to laugh, cry or yawn are all common. Some of you may feel a little hot after working with this strong energy flow, this is perfectly normal and is a nice way to validate the change in your personal energy.

After you have done this exercise for the first time and reactivated your Channel, you may do this exercise daily so that you really get your Channel back into great shape and keep it that way. I still use this technique regularly to keep my Channel strong. Remember, one visit to the gym is good, but only regular visits will give you the results you desire, and just as the condition of your body improves with regular exercise, so too will the condition of your Channel.

The following are recommended maintenance exercises that can be done daily to maintain excellent Channel energy flow. Choose the one that you like best or alternate them to give yourself some added variety.

GETTING MORE CONNECTED

EXERCISE FIVE

CHANNEL MAINTENANCE TECHNIQUE: BREATHING

REQUIREMENTS: a quiet location where you can sit or lie comfortably

TIME REQUIRED: 5–10 minutes

- As with the previous exercise choose a quiet location and sit or lie comfortably.
- Begin by inhaling deeply. As you do so, visualise bringing the nurturing energy of the Earth up through your feet, legs and body and then let it continue all the way up into the sky.
- With your out breath visualise energy and light travelling down from the Universe via your Channel and through your entire body length, back down into the Earth.
- Do this several times and imagine that each inhalation and exhalation draws in more of this energy and light, helping to clear, expand and strengthen your Channel.
- Repeat this exercise in reverse, drawing energy and light from the Universe on your in breath and letting the Earth fill you up on the out breath.

Eventually you will be able to feel the energy moving in both directions simultaneously no matter where you are in your own breath cycle. This constant two-way flow is how your Channel functions naturally, and serves to keep you Divinely Guided and grounded all at the same time.

EXERCISE SIX

CHANNEL MAINTENANCE TECHNIQUE: COLOUR AND LIGHT

REQUIREMENTS: a quiet location where you can sit or lie comfortably

TIME REQUIRED: 5–10 minutes

- Make yourself comfortable and close your eyes.
- Visualise your Channel of pure white light.
- When you are ready let your Channel be filled with a rich bright colour. The first colour that comes to you will be fine.
- Imagine this colour flowing down through your Channel from above, cleansing and strengthening it as it flows, letting it travel all the way to your feet and down into the Earth. Feel yourself being energised and uplifted by this wonderful, healing light, and ask that it bring you the Divine Guidance and spiritual connection you desire.
- Feel this coloured light come travelling back up through your Channel from the Earth, creating the continuous two-way flow. Remind yourself of your intention of clearing and strengthening your Channel by doing this exercise and that is what will be done.

When it comes to the choice of colour you are free to go with whatever you like. Many people see their favourite colours first, while others are drawn to colours that have a certain meaning for them. If you always see green for instance, it could be that you need help with matters of the heart because green is the main colour of the heart chakra, or it may simply be that green is a soothing and healing colour for you at that time. Try not to analyse these things too much and just let the healing powers of the energy and Light do the work for you.

In my private work brilliant gold and silver are colours I am often guided to use by my Angels. They have shown me many times how beneficial these powerful colours are for the purposes of healing and strengthening. When a client is particularly fatigued I am often guided to use an energy that reminds me of champagne! It is a soft golden colour and wonderfully sparkling and fresh, it's a great treat to give yourself when you are feeling a bit worn out.

In the end though, it is hard to go past a full rainbow. This is one of my favourites and is a delightful energy to work with. As you are practicing visualising and working on your Channel simply call in a rainbow so that you may benefit from all the healing colours of the spectrum at once. Imagine a rainbow flowing in to the top of your head and down through the length of your Channel, allowing the individual colours to move through you correcting any imbalances and dissolving any blockages as it goes.

Use one of these techniques for a few minutes each day and your Channel will remain strong and clear. Each time you practice you will be fine-tuning your ability to receive your Divine Guidance in the many forms that it comes. Your chakras will benefit enormously too of course, and it will help you to feel refreshed and relaxed.

Now that you have set up the basics of your spiritual anatomy it is time to work on the really exciting part . . . activating your Inner Screen.

Activating your inner screen

Your Inner Screen is connected to your brow chakra and its function in facilitating clairvoyant sight.

The Inner Screen is a useful device because it gives your conscious mind something to focus on. Just closing your eyes and hoping for something to appear might be okay for some, but if you actually allow an Inner Screen to be formally created, your mind can go back to it each time with a positive and expectant air.

Remember, your intention is very important and creating an Inner Screen sets a clear intention of choosing to develop your clairvoyant sight once more.

EXERCISE SEVEN

CREATING THE INNER SCREEN

REQUIREMENTS: a quiet location where you can sit or lie comfortably

TIME REQUIRED: 10–15 minutes

- Close your eyes and focus on the inner surface of your brow.

- Let a stream of colour or light flow to this area and create a large, clear screen there for you inside your forehead. Don't try to see anything on your screen at this time, just imagine it being created and prepared for you in the most perfect way.

- Some of you will notice that this area feels thick or cloudy, because just like your Channel, the Inner Screen can become overwhelmed with worry, emotions and the clutter and clatter of our minds. Ask the flow of colour and light to come and clear all of these obstructions away so that you can resurrect your clear Inner Screen.

- Utilise your imagination to help you picture a big white movie screen or flat screen plasma television on which you'll be able to see your images. Whenever I take a group of people through this exercise there is always a wonderful variety of Inner Screens.

- Have fun putting your Inner Screen together. Perhaps you imagine an elegant hand wiping the inner surface of your brow clear and clean. Or a cool breeze blowing away the old fog that the rational mind keeps in place in the form of scepticism, disbelief or lack of confidence in your own abilities. You could even invite a famous person to come and unveil it by pulling a cord and drawing aside that inner curtain!

- There is no right or wrong way to do this as such, so follow what feels good for you and trust that it is being done. In the beginning it is difficult to see images like this clearly in your mind, so set your intention, give it your full attention and do the best you can.
- Once you have cleaned your Inner Screen slowly open your eyes and reconnect with your real environment knowing that your Inner Screen is clear and ready to receive as needed.
- Allow yourself to feel confident that your Inner Screen is now clear and ready to help you develop your clairvoyant sight.

It is at this point that I would like to emphasise how important these simple exercises are. None of them need to take very long, a couple of minutes a day can achieve wonders.

As you become more proficient you will be able to strengthen and clear your Channel, Inner Screen and chakras at a moments notice, whether you are sitting on a train or bus or taking a few minutes for yourself in the office.

Quiet time at home or in a meditation group is the ideal time and place, but if you are always 'too busy' then you must make time whenever you can. Your spiritual anatomy is similar to your physical anatomy in one very important way. If you look after it, use it and treat it well it will remain healthy and strong and pay you back a thousandfold for your efforts.

FURTHER READING ON THIS SUBJECT:

Wheels of Light by Rosalyn L. Bruyere
Hands of Light by Barbara Ann Brennan
Anatomy of the Spirit by Caroline Myss

CHAPTER 5

Meeting your Angels and Spirit Guides

'Thanks again for the reading today. It has not left my mind even for a minute. I am revelling in the reality that I have an Angel of my own. Not one but two. To say that they have been looking over me all this time and that they love me unconditionally seemed important. I can't keep from crying at some points because it feels like suddenly, after so much time of feeling alone, I am no longer alone, and I would never have guessed that I would roll over that easy. I am a sceptic after all.'

ROBERT M.

In my experience it is a rare person who isn't at least a little bit intrigued by the idea of meeting one of their Angels or Spirit Guides. I am fortunate enough to have travelled a great deal and wherever I go I meet people who are hungry for more information on this subject.

Some people already have a strong belief about the existence of their unseen friends, others have felt a loving presence around them before, particularly during a difficult time in their lives. It is natural for many more people to be sceptical, after all, we live in a world where physical or actual proof that something exists is usually the minimum standard.

Recently I had the good fortune to go to Rome and enjoy the monumental and beautiful works of art that cover the walls and ceilings of the Vatican buildings and the Sistine Chapel. It struck me then how Angels have long been depicted in art, but usually in scenes of great drama, triumph or religious significance. Perhaps the underlying message that we have taken from this is that Angels only come to you if you are someone special, or that they belong only in the mythologies of certain religions. Thankfully today we are broadening our view to the point where thousands of people are now happy to confess their interest in and experiences with their Angels and Spirit Guides.

Many people ask me what the difference is between Spirit Guides, Angels, Archangels and Ascended Masters, as they are the four 'levels' of beings that I most commonly Channel during the readings.

The way it has been explained and shown to me over the years is that each of these groups live in a different dimension or vibration. The vibration that the Spirit Guides live in is closest to our dimension here on Earth, or to put it another way, it has a similar frequency.

All Spirit Guides have lived on Earth before as human beings, giving them a profound understanding of what our experiences here are like. When we are born we have some Spirit Guides with us, some of whom will stay with us for the duration of our lives and some who will only be here for the time it takes to help us to get the most from certain human experiences we came here to understand. Therefore the number of Spirit Guides that a person can have with them at any one time will vary, as new ones come in and old ones leave, depending on where you are at with your life.

I can vividly recall the positive effect that connecting with a Spirit Guide had for one of my clients who was going through a difficult time. In her mid-30s and never married, this lady was devastated by the death of both her parents within the same year. When she first came to see me she felt very alone, and realised that she had given little thought or energy to getting married herself as her parents and her career had always been of paramount importance to her.

She often cried herself to sleep at night, wondering when it would be her turn and realising that her inherent shyness had caused her to avoid making contact with eligible men. Her somewhat sheltered life had changed forever and she needed help.

She had a general sense of her Spirit Guides from her first session with me, so we called on them again and asked them for help. Soon after, as she lay crying in bed one night, she felt a warm presence surround her and a sense of calm descend in her mind. She reported a soothing sensation as though someone were stroking the side of her face lovingly and brushing the hair from her tear-streaked face, it was very comforting and reassuring for her.

This experience continued most nights for the next few months and feeling lonely in her empty home, she spoke to this Spirit Guide and told him of her feelings and fears. She came to think of him as Tom, was very clear that he was a male and could describe his appearance. As she recovered from her grief she also came to think of him as a constant friend.

Then one day this woman realised that she had not seen Tom for quite a while. Her life had become so busy and it had been several months since she had given her Spirit Guides and Angels any thought at all. She felt a bit guilty about this as she remembered how much Tom's visits had meant to her, and on thinking about it further she realised that he had not shown himself since something very special had happened in her life.

During these last few months she had finally begun to notice the attentions of a man she worked with. He had always been very nice to her, but she never thought much of it. One day he asked her out for lunch and during their conversation it suddenly hit her. She liked him so much and always had, but had remained closed to him.

The relationship blossomed rapidly from there and soon they were engaged, and both truly delighted. It suddenly occurred to her that Tom had been there to help her through that lonely time after her parents' death and to listen to her feelings about wanting her own relationship and family.

Our connection with our Spirit Guides and Angels can be funny in that way, we might only think of them when we are in trouble and then 'forget' them when the problem is solved. They don't mind, because they understand that emotional pain is a bit like physical pain, you don't notice the part of you that is hurting after the pain is gone.

Because your Spirit Guides come and go, so to speak, it is always worth checking in from time to time to see who is with you. I was recently introduced to a new one of my own, and working with him and getting to know him has been delightful.

Many, but not all, Angels, so they tell me, have also lived on Earth. Those who haven't lived here still have the gift of empathy and relate to us very well. All Angels bring a wider perspective of understanding to our lives. The vibration, frequency or dimension that they dwell in is of a higher tone. This doesn't mean to say that they are better than Spirit Guides or humans, but they have a different view and understanding. It is common for Angels to let a client know that they are learning just as much from us as we are from them.

We benefit our Angels by allowing them to help us because that is an important part of their mission. In my experience, the number of Angels with any one person remains consistent throughout their lifetime, with some Angels taking a more prominent role at various times. Our Angels have known us since before we were born and helped us to choose the kind of incarnation that would be of most benefit to our soul's purpose in this life.

Naturally, they are also here to help us, but unless our parents were enlightened enough to teach us about their presence, most of us completely forget about our Angels by the time we reach puberty.

Your parents were probably inclined to tell you that it was just your imagination when you reported the awareness of one of your Angels as a child. Fortunately this trend is changing as more adults come to experience Angelic presence as truth, and help to keep this knowledge alive in their children.

There doesn't seem to be any limit to the number of Spirit Guides or Angels that you can have in your personal group, some people have a veritable crowd around them, but you will certainly have all that you need whether you are aware of them or not.

Archangels and Ascended Masters inhabit different realms again and having been Angels and/or Spirit Guides in previous incarnations, they are very experienced and powerful. Both of these groups are omnipresent, which means that they are available to anyone and everyone at all times. These beings are of such a high vibration that just thinking about one of them can bring comfort and give your own 'vibe' a boost.

The Archangels Michael, Gabriel, Raphael and Uriel are familiar to most of you by name at least, but there are many more. The Ascended Masters are an impressive group including among them no less than Mother Mary, Mary Magdalene, Jesus (Lord Sananda), Joseph of Arimathea, Saint Germaine, Lady Nada and Lord Kuthumi. For the purposes of this book however, we will focus only on your own personal group; that is your Spirit Guides and Angels; you can do your own research into the Archangels and Ascended Masters.

Over the years I have spoken to many people who felt that they had been protected or saved by a force outside of themselves when they were placed in a dangerous situation. One man I met a long time ago had a horrendous car accident in the New Zealand countryside. A split second before the accident happened he saw a brilliant flash of light and had a profound feeling that everything was going to be all right despite the chaos that happened all around him.

The memory of that light helped him to remain positive and strong as he went through his long recovery. Ultimately he came to understand that the changes the accident had brought about in his life were positive, and he felt extremely thankful.

I have also had a number of encounters with helpful Angels who came to comfort or help me. One such visit happened only a few years ago; by which time I was already very accustomed to having them around. It was a very hot summer, early February if my memory serves me right, and a friend in Brisbane was unable to locate his very old and feeble cat.

This cat was a beloved pet, close to 20 years old. It was not handling the 40 degree-plus heatwave at all well. It was about 10 pm when my friend phoned me to say that he had searched *everywhere* for this cat and was extremely worried, he didn't want her to suffer.

My clairvoyant sight revealed nothing to me, we chatted for a while, said our farewells and I went off to bed. After lying with my eyes closed for around 15 minutes I felt an urge to open my eyes and at the end of my bed stood three enormous Angels. They were of a soft, whitish, cloud-like outline, all of them male and very strong looking, very masculine. Instinctively I felt that they were the Archangels Gabriel, Raphael and Michael and the energy of their presence was calming, reassuring and wonderful.

The whole meeting lasted no more than 10 seconds. I watched them as they stood there looking not so much at me, but more like through or around me. Immediately I had a strong feeling that my friend's cat would be found alive and well; the Angels then disappeared and off to sleep I went.

The following morning a very excited email came to let me know that he had found his cat sleeping under the house, in a place my friend thought he had already searched, 20 to 30 minutes after we ended our phone conversation. I was delighted of course, and had yet another good reason to say thanks to the Angels.

Okay, I know you are keen to discover how it is you can connect with your wonderful friends. The following exercise is simple, effective and a great way to meet with your Angels and Spirit Guides.

Before you start the exercise make it your clear intention that this is what you want. If the idea of having Angels and Spirit Guides around you is completely new to you then you may even feel a little bit nervous, but there is nothing to worry about. Make it your intention to connect with these Beings who love you and have your best interests at heart.

Make sure that you have done all the previous exercises from chapter four at least once before moving on to this process.

This book is presented in a certain order for a reason, so until you have done each exercise at least once it is best that you follow the sequence as it is presented, just as you would do if you were taking one of my courses and learning something new each week in class.

After you have done them all, starting with the chakra maintenance, Channel and Inner Screen activations from chapter four, then you can pick and choose which exercises appeal to you most and focus more upon them.

I also recommend that you get yourself a notebook or journal in which you can keep a record of the experiences you will have and the information you will receive. It's easy to forget the details when your mind gets busy again, and far too easy to lose the well meaning scrap of paper you scribbled on. Treat yourself to a lovely book to record your adventures; it will be well worth it.

EXERCISE EIGHT

MEET ONE OF YOUR ANGELS OR SPIRIT GUIDES

REQUIREMENTS: a quiet place where

you can sit or lie comfortably

Pen

Notebook or Journal

TIME REQUIRED: 10–20 minutes

- First sit or lie down somewhere that you can be comfortable, take the phone off the hook, put the 'Do Not Disturb' sign out, anything you need to ensure you won't be interrupted. It is probably best not to do this in bed because the object of this exercise is not to fall asleep, nor is it necessarily to relax, you want to be calm and focused and ready to connect.

- Spend a couple of minutes doing the Channel activation process from chapter four, so that you know your Channel is open and strong. Remember, your Channel is your antennae for your Divine Guidance, so the more exercise you give it, the better it will work for you.

- Place your pen and notebook within reach.

- Now close your eyes and take a moment to consider your intention, the reason you are doing this exercise – to meet one of your Spirit Guides or Angels.

- Imagine yourself travelling up into the sky, floating or flying, you leave your room behind and fly up through the sky, going higher and higher. Imagine the clouds as you pass them by, feeling happy, free and full of excited anticipation.

- Imagine your Channel to be like a kind of guide rope that guides you on your journey up into Space while still keeping you safely connected to planet Earth.

- Soon you have risen so far that you begin to leave the Earth's atmosphere and are moving out into space.

- Picture yourself going past our beautiful moon and out past the planets in our solar system such as Venus, Jupiter, Neptune and Pluto. Make your journey as colourful and interesting as you like, there is no need to rush; stop and study the awesome and colourful rings of Saturn or to marvel at the comets and asteroids as they glide on by.

Note: If you want to be really thorough you can take the time to look at an atlas of astronomy or the internet to familiarise yourself with the celestial geography before you head off, so you can picture where you are going with greater ease.

- Continue to travel upward into the Cosmos, holding your clear intention in your mind that you are on a journey to meet one of your Angels or Spirit Guides. Soon you will leave our Solar System and find yourself in the vastness of Space where you will continue to travel for a minute or two longer, enjoying the incredible peace of the Universe and the brilliance of the stars.

- When you feel ready, allow yourself to come to a stop and to simply float or hover in Space with stars and planets moving slowly around you.

- Pause for a moment and let yourself feel the security of the guideline and anchor that your Channel provides for you.

- Now that you have become a little bit accustomed to just 'hanging out' in Space look straight ahead into the distance and imagine a small but very bright point of light. Let this light come closer and closer towards you. It travels with great speed and accuracy, becoming larger all the while.

- Eventually it is right there before you, only a few feet away and so very bright that you may feel the urge to shield your eyes. Remind yourself that you are here to meet a Spirit Guide or Angel, a meeting that, one way or another, you have been looking forward to all of your life. You will soon notice that the intensity of this mass of light begins to soften a little so that you are able to look directly at it.

- As you watch, a form will begin to reveal itself to you; there is nothing you have to do other than just observe. Just relax and allow your Angel or Spirit Guide to come to you, be receptive and welcoming and notice whatever shows up.

- You may get a sense of whether it is male or female, or notice part or all of his or her appearance, and so on. In your mind's eye let the image of your Angel or Spirit Guide be shown to you and keep asking for more information. It is perfectly acceptable to ask as many questions as you like, especially if you are not very visual at this time.

- Ask your friend what colour their eyes are, what s/he is wearing, what her/his name is or whether s/he is an Angel or a Spirit Guide. Even if you can't 'see' this being, you will feel it, because their energy feels warm and wonderful, so you may want to reach out to hold hands or give and receive a hug.

- Keep examining your Spirit Guide or Angel until you have gathered all the information about them that you feel you can at this time. Trust what you sense and let the impressions flow freely; your friend can have any name and any kind of appearance, not all Angels have flowing robes and golden wings and Spirit Guides appear in a truly limitless variety.

- When you feel that you have spent enough time reuniting with your friend you can then make your journey back to Earth; this time with your Spirit Guide or Angel by your side.

- Using your Channel as a guiding line again, travel back down along it through the stars, into our Solar System and back into the Earth's atmosphere. Picture yourself descending gently and gracefully with your Spirit Guide or Angel by your side and going directly back to wherever you began your journey from.

- Make your journey back logical and sequential, coming back the same way you went out, then returning to the country, city, town, suburb, street, home or building, and then finally the room you set out from. Affirm to yourself the present place and time, for example, your street address and the date; breathe deeply, wriggle your fingers and toes, feel the weight of your body in the chair, and then open your eyes. You are back where you started and your Angel or Spirit Guide is now there beside you.

- Now before you do anything else, take your pen and notebook and write down every little detail you can remember, including their name if you got one. It really helps to make a note of these things when you are in the early stages of this work because it is all too easy to leap back into your busy day and forget half of what you experienced.

This whole process need only take a few minutes if that is what you want, but if you can spare the time it is worthwhile giving yourself around half an hour so you can savour and enjoy it.

VARIATION

Another simple visualisation to meet your Angel or Spirit Guide is outlined below. You can alternate between the two versions or choose your favourite visualisation style.

REQUIREMENTS: a quiet place where you can sit or lie comfortably, Pen and Notebook or Journal

TIME REQUIRED: 10–20 minutes

- Sit or lie down comfortably in a relaxed, private place.

- Spend a few minutes doing the Channel connection exercise from chapter four so that you know that your Channel is open and strong.

- Place your pen and notebook nearby.

- Now close your eyes and spend a couple of minutes considering your intention, the reason you are doing this exercise – to meet one of your Angels or Spirit Guides.

- Remind yourself that your celestial team is always with you, even if you have not been aware of them up until now. Just relax and breathe deeply as you invite your Angels and Spirit Guides to come in close and form a loving circle around you.

- Imagine them forming this circle around you. Don't struggle to see or feel anything, just be with the experience as it unfolds. Keep inviting them in and let them know that they are welcome.

- As they gather around you it's possible to feel emotional, warm, like the atmosphere has changed in the room. Be open and keep inviting them in.

- Then ask one of your group to make themselves more clearly known to you by stepping forward, connecting more clearly.

You may feel as though someone has stepped in closer, laid a loving hand on your shoulder or knelt down in front of you; some people feel a cool breeze or a caress on the side of their face.

- Then ask these simple questions and listen for a response with your heart, just accept the first impressions that comes to you rather than trying to analyse it. Ask – Are you an Angel or Spirit Guide? Are you masculine or feminine? What do you look like? What is your name?

- Stay relaxed and repeat the questions if you would like to, but don't try to force anything. Tune in, be open and feel the responses rather than expect a certain style of reply.

- If you'd like to add another question you can ask – Do you have a message for me? Or – Are you here to help me with or teach me something in particular?

- Then imagine reaching out and receiving a hug from your Angel or Spirit Guide.

- Let them indicate to you a beautiful golden pathway, the pathway of your highest truth in this life. Then, linking arms or holding hands with your Angel or Spirit Guide, allow yourself to move forward on your pathway with their love and support, knowing that you don't have to go it alone.

- Let the whole scene be enveloped in beautiful Light. Whatever colour comes to you is fine. Thank your Angels and Spirit Guides for being with you, thank the one you connected with today for his or her love and support. Then commit to staying in closer contact with them from now on.

- Sit with these beautiful feelings for a moment longer, then slowly open your eyes. Take a nice deep breath, feel the warm energy that surrounds you and write down everything you can remember in your notebook as you savour your experience.

If at any time during the process you feel that you have drifted off, then just pick up where you left off. There is no right or wrong way to do this, so you may add your own variations if you like. Some people like to imagine that they are walking into a beautiful forest, stopping in a clearing or a grove to meet their new friend. If you have a favourite place or setting you would prefer to use, then by all means do so, no one method is better than the other, what is most important is that it works for you.

Normally, you will meet just one Angel or Spirit Guide each time you make this trip, but it is possible to be greeted by two or more. There are no rules, so be open to surprises and trust yourself and what you are being shown.

Keep asking the ones you connect with for the names they go by; I find it is much easier for people to relate to an Angel or Spirit Guide if they have a name to address them by. There doesn't seem to be any names that are typical, in my years of practice I have come across Spirit Guides and Angels with names ranging from the very ordinary, like Bob and Jane, to the unusual, like Wohan and Erethelia.

Once you have made contact there is no need to repeat that process again for the same Angel or Spirit Guide, but do repeat it whenever you would like to meet other members of your clan. If you are going through a difficult time, or want help with something specific, you can ask to meet the Being who can most particularly help you with that problem. You may then be guided to a new one or be shown one of your known Angels or Spirit Guides who can help you with that.

Staying in touch with your Guides

Getting to know your Angels or Guides better is simple too. Develop your relationship with them by talking to them in your mind. Start your day by inviting them to join you and be close to you, say 'Good morning Erethelia, thank you for this wonderful day, please come and be close by my side throughout the day and please help me with . . .' and so on.

Ask your Angels and Spirit Guides to reveal more about themselves to you in your relaxed and quiet times. Make time to sit and commune with them or contemplate them as you are drifting off to sleep; and if you didn't get a name during that initial process then keep asking for it and it will come to you eventually.

Your Angels and Spirit Guides want to have a closer relationship with you, so tell them about yourself, your life, how you feel and what you dream of. It's all about getting reacquainted with a long lost friend, there is a lot of catching up to do, so don't hold back.

Messages from your new friends can come to you in all sorts of ways. Say for instance you are getting frustrated because you can't seem to determine your Angel's name. If you expect the name to come to you like some booming voice in your head then you may be missing the point. Sure, the booming voice thing can happen, just like it does in the movies, but what is more likely is that you will have a feeling or a sense of a name, a more subtle impression rather than something that knocks you off your chair.

Your celestial friends will also use everyday items and situations to communicate with you, it's important to be observant, like my client who kept asking her Angel for his name. In frustration she rang me and said 'Maybe he doesn't want to tell me his name', and then she went off to work.

That day in the office the name Daniel kept coming to her from all over the place. She was introduced to someone called Daniel, two customer enquiries that she had to deal with were from people called Daniel and then finally, as she was driving home, the car in front of her in the slow moving, peak hour traffic had a customised number plate with the letters DAN on it. She finally got it and laughed about it all the way home.

Your Angels and Spirit Guides will find all sorts of interesting and creative ways to communicate with you and to help you to develop your faith in their presence. They have an amazing sense of timing and humour, with an approach that will often serve to remind us to slow down and enjoy life rather than be constantly rushing around getting things done. One of their most commonly acknowledged methods is to leave feathers in the most unusual places for you, like a calling card to remind you that they are around, or a feather lying in a fairly normal location like a park will really stand out to you.

Their messages can come to you in any way, shape or form, so be observant and don't be surprised if a song you have heard a thousand times suddenly holds new meaning for you, or people keep mentioning similar ideas or themes to you in their conversation, or the headline on the next magazine or newspaper you pick up makes sense to you in a very personal way. They will use whatever means are at hand because they know all too well that our minds are often too busy to clearly hear messages in a spoken form.

Over time you will learn to notice and respond to the more subtle forms of contact like that inner feeling or nudge that your Angels or Spirit Guides will give you to help you make the most positive choices for yourself. Tuning into these subtle messages takes practice and a willingness to be patient with yourself as you learn to let go of the lifelong habit of overriding your intuitive feelings.

It is important to realise that even though we have a lot of different languages here on Earth, the Universe doesn't communicate in any of them as such. The real language of the soul is one of feeling, so if it feels right then believe it and act on it and when it doesn't feel right then don't. It really is that simple.

One of the most effective ways to allow your Angels and Spirit Guides to help you is to speak to them from a place of intention and empowerment. The old approach of asking for something in a 'Please give me this; please make such and such happen; or please do this and that for me' is no longer very effective.

As part of humanity's overall evolutionary process we are being encouraged to take responsibility and control over the creation of our own reality. There is no 'God' on high, dispensing wishes to some and not to others. We need to learn to take responsibility for the fact that we create and attract most of what we experience in our lives.

To this end, a much better way of making 'requests' of any kind is to word it this way:

'Dear Angels, what do I need to do or not do, start or stop, understand, embrace or let go of, in order to bring this into my life, in order to have this experience? What can I do to help this desired event come about, how can I allow myself to receive (whatever it is you are asking for).'

Do you notice the difference? You are not making a passive plea for help and expecting the Universe to sort it all out for you. You are activating the powerful energy of your intention and indicating to your Spirit Guides, Angels and the Universe that you are willing to do your share and meet halfway.

When you communicate with your celestial friends in this way it gives them much greater scope to help you by creating situations and opportunities that bring your wishes to life. In this way you will be co-creating your life with their help, and have the chance to make changes and choices that will help you to refine the outcome.

Becoming more intuitive and psychic is not about waiting around for someone else to fix your life for you; it's about working with your helpers to develop your own innate skills and strengths as the powerful, spiritually aware being that you are and are becoming.

You can use this method to request help with less tangible matters as well. You may, for instance, wish to develop qualities that you feel you lack, such as courage, compassion, confidence or faith in yourself. To ask your Angels 'How can I develop a greater faith in myself? What do I need to do or not do, learn or let go of?' etc. is a very empowering experience and will generate some incredible opportunities for you.

At first, you may not recognise your Angels' response to your request until you look back and think 'Wow! I felt really strong in that situation, and stuck to my guns. That was a great opportunity to develop my faith in myself!'

One last advantage of working with your Spirit Guides and Angels in this way is you find out very quickly what you *really* want. It is all very well to bombard your Angels with a shopping list and say 'Give me this, this, this and this', but when you bring yourself into the equation and acknowledge that you have to meet the Universe halfway and act in your own best interests, you soon weed out the things that aren't so important to you. This then frees you to focus on what you *really* desire for yourself and your life. You will find that when a genuine request is made from the heart, with a willingness to participate, the Universe always responds.

Remember Robert M. who wrote about his experience of meeting his Angels at the beginning of this chapter? Well, he has since moved back to the United States, and here is what he has to say nearly two years later:

> *That first meeting with my Angels was a very powerful experience for me. Within a few weeks of that first reading, my breathing difficulties stopped as well as the associated general feelings of anxiety . . . It gave me a much better appreciation of my personality in this life, and through a more complete understanding, I was able to more fully pursue the person I wanted to be. It was as if I suddenly took a leap forward in my understanding of the universe, and more importantly, how I fit into that picture . . .*
>
> **ROBERT M.**

FURTHER READING ON THIS SUBJECT:

A Little Light on Angels by Diana Cooper
Angel Therapy by Doreen Virtue
Archangels and Ascended Masters by Doreen Virtue
Website: www.crystalinks.com a great resource for all subjects in this book, including *Angels and Ascended Masters*.

CHAPTER 6

How to conduct a psychic conversation

'Every time I mentioned going on a cruise my wife became agitated, upset and even angry, so I had a Psychic Conversation with her about it. A couple of days later she came to me and told me the idea of a cruise terrified her, but she had felt silly telling me. Having that Psychic Conversation with my wife helped us to get to the truth of the matter.'

G.D.

I don't know about you, but throughout my life I have found it difficult at times to communicate my true feelings to someone. Fortunately I have usually been able to let someone know when I like, love and appreciate them; though maybe not often enough. What I am talking about are those difficult conversations, where the subject matter is tricky or liable to trigger some kind of disagreement or conflict.

Like most people, I would rather run a mile across burning hot coals than face a confrontation with someone. For much of my life I felt intimidated by most people, *especially* those people who I perceived to have a temper and capable of expressing their anger openly to or at me. This was terrifying stuff for me and I would avoid it at all costs; but as we know, this does not usually lead to a resolution and can often make matters worse.

Ideally I guess it would be wonderful if we could all be composed and courageous enough to take our concerns or confusion directly to the person involved and discuss it with them face to face. We have all beaten ourselves up in the past for not being 'more adult' about things. If you feel this way remind yourself that verbal and even written communication is known to be only partially effective and is very open to misinterpretation.

This is where the technique of the Psychic Conversation can be extremely useful because it is a tool which can help you communicate with other people effectively and gently.

The term 'psychic' in this case does not refer to someone with a gift for reading the future or tapping into another person's thoughts or beliefs. What it refers to is a mode of communication other than a physical or verbal one. It refers to the fact that we communicate with each other on much more subtle levels all the time, mostly without even knowing it. In fact, observers and researchers in the field of human communication have long acknowledged that speaking to each other constitutes only around 10 per cent of all human communications.

We communicate much more eloquently with each other through our body language, our facial expressions, our actions and our *thoughts*. If you believe that you can be angry or upset with someone and hide it from them because you haven't actually told them about it, then you are fooling yourself. Human beings are incredibly sensitive, and even if the object of your anger or hurt can't accurately describe the vibe you are giving off they will know that something is amiss.

A Psychic Conversation is effective because you are not only communicating with words and thoughts, but also with feelings. It doesn't matter what language you speak or what generation you are from, as human beings we all understand the power and energy of feelings because they bypass our mind, which is likely to filter and interpret them, and they reach us in our heart and our gut.

Psychic Conversations are also a great help when the person you want to communicate with lives far away. Phone calls, letters, emails and the like are notorious for being open to misinterpretation over long distances and/or when you haven't seen the person for quite some time.

So if you quail at the idea of fronting up to a certain person with a request or a problem, if you know that your voice will shake or your bottom lip will quiver or that you are liable to burst into tears and forget half the things you wanted to say, don't feel bad. You are not being weak, you are simply being human.

Or if like me, you sometimes find yourself suffering from a bad case of 'foot-in-mouth' disease when you are trying to communicate your feelings, then help is at hand. All of us are sensitive to the reactions and opinions of others and getting the words to come out right under pressure can be difficult.

The world sometimes seems full of people who would like us to believe that they can intimidate us into having things their way. The wonderful thing about Psychic Conversations is that it allows you to approach someone that you might even be afraid of, and get a positive result. It can turn supposed enemies into friends, intimidators into supporters, resolve issues with people who no longer belong in your life so you can let them go, and give you a sense of inner strength that you did not previously know you had.

However the Psychic Conversation technique is not about forcing others to come around to your point of view. It is about giving yourself the best possible opportunity of expressing your truth clearly, without the interruption or even derision that you may fear. The Psychic Conversation was taught to me by my Angels and Guides many years ago, not as a tool to be used upfront, before I had given the other person a chance, but to be used when all my other attempts at communicating my feelings or needs had failed. When it was very clear that the other person would not be open to my point of view.

It is not a tool that you can use to manipulate others; it cannot influence them unfairly to do what you want, it is simply another way of communicating with someone, a way that most of us have forgotten or are reluctant to acknowledge.

By having a Psychic Conversation with someone, you are able to communicate with them on a very deep and direct level, and you will be able to express yourself clearly and fully without fear of interruption or negative reaction.

Once I learned the technique of the Psychic Conversation I realised that I had been having lesser versions of these types of conversations with people all my life. We all do it.

Just think about this for a moment. If someone upsets you, is keeping something from you, forgets your birthday or wedding anniversary or something like that, what do you do? Chances are you will play the scene over in your head countless times, imagining yourself handling the situation with more courage or calm. You will re-run a type of conversation in your mind, going over how you feel and what you want, usually going around in circles until you are fed up with the whole thing, and yet after all this effort and stress on your part the situation remains unresolved. This is a disempowering process because you are doing it from a place of powerlessness. All you are doing is chewing on the angst that you feel and making matters worse for yourself. Learning how to conduct a Psychic Conversation will change all of that.

The Psychic Conversation utilises the incredible power of our conscious and subconscious minds to create a constructive communication that is honouring and respectful for all involved. By focusing your attention on the person and the difficulty at hand, you can resolve situations that may otherwise remain stuck for long periods of time. The Psychic Conversation gives you the opportunity to communicate with others at the level of the heart, a level of much greater openness and deeper understanding, and because you are able to concentrate fully on your own feelings and what you want to communicate, it is a very effective process.

Often when we try to communicate with others in the ordinary ways – verbally or in writing – we encounter barriers constructed by that person at the level of the ego and conscious mind. For better or for worse we have all grown up to believe that we have to defend our corner in life and that understanding another's needs or point of view is a form of weakness, or leaves us open to losing in some way.

Growing up in a complex and competitive world our defences are strong; *all* of us have and use them. The Psychic Conversation is not about drumming in to the other person that you are right and they are wrong, it is a tool to be used respectfully so that you can express your true feelings without censure or interruption.

My Angels taught me a 'three strikes you're out' policy with Psychic Conversations and I believe that this is a useful lesson. If you have the same Psychic Conversation with the same person three times and still get no response, then it is time to accept that they are simply not interested in your point of view, and move on. You have used the tool with integrity, expressed your feelings clearly, described in detail the outcome you would like, but what the person on the receiving end does with this communication is always up to them. We are all beings of free will and we are not here to spend our time and energy trying to force others to bend to ours; by acknowledging the 'three strikes you're out' policy you are showing that you are humble and flexible enough to let go and move on.

The Psychic Conversation technique has brought me some amazing responses and results and has proven to me without a doubt that we can communicate with others at the level of thought, without even being in the same country, city or room.

After conducting a Psychic Conversation with the person in question I have received phone calls or bumped into them on the street, sometimes after not having seen them for years. Not only have they contacted me, but have then initiated a discussion about the exact topic of my concern. Sometimes coming forth with an apology or offering important information, depending on what I asked for as the outcome.

A classic example is my experience of being awarded a pay rise in my job during my time in the fashion industry. My boss had made it clear to all of us that no pay rises would be forthcoming in the foreseeable future, but I knew that compared to my colleagues, I was being considerably underpaid. I found my boss very intimidating in those days, and there was no way that I was game to broach this subject with him, but after conducting two Psychic Conversations with him on this topic a miracle happened.

About a week after the second conversation I was summoned to his office. I had no idea what this meeting was going to be about as I had forgotten about my Psychic Conversation efforts. You can imagine my surprise and delight when he told me I would be receiving a pay rise. He made it very clear to me that I was to tell nobody about it as company policy was not permitting pay rises at this time, but he had been aware that I had been working hard, had started on a lower salary than my peers due to my initial lack of experience in that role, and that I had not had a pay rise since starting with the company. My boss had gotten permission from the owner of the company to give me a rise of $5000 a year!

I was thrilled and could barely suppress my urge to laugh at the time. It was hard to keep my good news to myself, but I thanked my Angels a hundred times that day for their help. My Psychic Conversation with my boss had worked, the evidence could not be denied.

Another striking example was during a time when I was dating a man I was quite besotted by. He was an instructor at my gym, and with the benefit of hindsight I might say now that I should have known better.

We dated for a while and it was all very nice, but after a couple of months I couldn't shake the feeling that something wasn't right. He would behave a bit strangely from time to time, get phone calls at odd hours that seemed to vex him and would sometimes cancel a date at very short notice.

Naturally I wasn't impressed and had tried to talk to him about it but he would just clam up or say I was overreacting. I had no actual proof of any deceit or wrongdoing, but my intuition told me something was very wrong. Now you need to remember that I really liked this guy at the time, and at the level of my ego I wanted to believe that everything was ok. He was a gym instructor and personal trainer after all . . . a busy guy always in demand!

Some of my friends were suspicious of his behaviour but most of them believed that I was reading too much into things and that I should just relax or be more patient. But finally I listened to my intuition and decided to have a Psychic Conversation with him in order to find out where I stood.

The outcome that I wanted was that he would be honest with me about what was going on in his life, so that I could make an informed choice about my involvement with him. Once again, the result was much better and swifter in coming than I had expected. He phoned me the following morning to say that he wanted to see me as soon as I was able. He came around to my place for a late breakfast and without any prompting he confessed all.

It turned out that he wasn't ready for a relationship at all, and that although he had been trying to start a relationship with me, he had not completely gotten over his previous girlfriend, and was still in the throws of trying to either patch things up or end it with her. It was complicated and messy and no woman ever feels terribly flattered by this kind of revelation. It's not a very glamorous thing to find out that you are the rebound girl, but at least I had the truth now and could end our relationship without any doubts in my mind.

Although it hurt to hear the truth at first, the Psychic Conversation had brought me a good result, as now I could make an informed decision and move on.

So, by now I hope you are bouncing up and down in your seats demanding 'How do I conduct one of these Psychic Conversations?'

Well, here's how. Read the instructions carefully and keep it simple. This is not a complicated process. The most important thing is that you are coming from a genuine place of integrity and have already tried discussing your concern with the person you want to have a Psychic Conversation with.

Your intention is everything, and is all important to receiving a positive and helpful response. If your intention is just to ram your opinion down the other person's throat, to blame them for your unhappiness and try to prove that you are right, then the Universe won't support you. The Psychic Conversation is not a place for righteous indignation or a cheap attempt at manipulating the will or behaviour of others. Make sure that your intention is purely to express your true feelings in a clear and honest manner.

On some occasions this will include feelings of anger or disappointment or letting the other person know that you didn't like what they did or said, but it is not about making them wrong, it is about owning your own feelings on the matter and creating this chance to express them.

EXERCISE NINE

CONDUCTING A PSYCHIC CONVERSATION

REQUIREMENTS: a quiet location where you can sit or lie comfortably

A clear intention

TIME REQUIRED: Approx. 20 minutes

- First of all decide who it is you want to talk to and what your main topic will be.

- Sit or lie somewhere quiet, comfortable and private and close your eyes. Calm your mind and focus on your intention, including the outcome you would like to have happen as a result of this conversation.

- Imagine yourself contacting this person in some way, by telephone for example, and calmly inform them that you wish to talk with them. Designate the time and place. Make sure it is a place where you feel very comfortable, confident and safe such as a favourite café, park or beach, or your own lounge room if you prefer. Anywhere that you can imagine talking with this person about your chosen topic is fine.

- Imagine them arriving just as you have instructed. Welcome them and have them place themselves wherever you want.

- Begin by clearly stating your topic, then tell them everything you have not been able to tell them so far. Imagine them sitting and listening to you respectfully and attentively; simply taking in what you are saying without reaction. Go into as much detail as you want and need to do. Say everything you need to say and get it all off your chest. This is your time to speak because you have created this opportunity to do it, so use it well.

- When you are completely finished, be sure to then say what outcome you want. You will have thought about this clearly before starting the Psychic Conversation, but if other ideas come to you while it is happening that's fine. Don't leave anything out. Would you like an apology? How about a phone call from that person or an offer to renew the friendship? Maybe you want to get back together with your partner and also had an apology to offer them during the conversation, or maybe it is a pay rise that you want. Make sure that your desired outcome is very clear.

- After you have completely expressed your feelings about your side of the situation and been clear about the outcome you would like, you can then thank them for coming and hearing you, and politely ask them to leave. The other person does not reply or respond, remember, they are a being of free will, so it is not for you to try to imagine what they might say at this time. This meeting was initiated by you and was your opportunity to talk.

- Once the person has 'left', continue to sit peacefully with your eyes closed for a few moments. Notice how you are feeling now that you have expressed yourself clearly and truthfully. Let that feeling sink in and then when you are ready, open your eyes.

- If you wish, jot down the details of who you spoke to, what you said and what outcome you requested.

After conducting a Psychic Conversation most people report that they feel a sense of relief or lightness because they have finally found a constructive way to release something that they have been carrying around inside themselves for a while.

Now it is up to the other person to respond and time for you to let go, because you cannot control them. The best thing you can do now is to forget all about the Psychic Conversation and get on with your life.

If you believe that you are dealing with someone who is particularly stubborn or resistant then you may have the same or similar conversation with them a total of three times.

Sometimes the response will come to you in ways that you hadn't imagined. You may well get the apology that you wanted for example, but it may come in the form of a letter or card, or through a third party, rather than in person or on the phone as you might have expected. Understand that you are learning a new way of communicating with people, and like all new skills this one will also benefit you more with practice, so be patient with yourself and allow space for your desired outcome to happen in miraculous ways.

One of the most striking memories I have of a Psychic Conversation helping one of my students is from years ago during one of the many meditation courses I used to run. This young woman was being hounded by her ex-boyfriend.

She had broken up with him several months before joining our group, but she was quiet in class and I knew nothing of her situation. On the night that I took the students through the Psychic Conversation technique she worked through the process like everyone else did, and then we all went home.

It was not my policy to inquire as to the content of each student's conversation, but only to help them with the process if they didn't understand something or felt stuck.

The following week we all gathered for class and I asked if anyone had a story to share since trying the Psychic Conversation technique for the first time. This gentle young woman offered to share hers.

Many of us were very troubled by her description of her ex-boyfriend's behaviour towards her. She had ended the relationship because he became verbally abusive when he drank alcohol. He would yell, slam doors and storm out and they had received many complaints from their neighbours. It had been hard for her to end it because when he was sober he promised it would never happen again and he would be 'on his best behaviour' for a while, but still refused to seek any professional help even though she had made it clear that she was willing to support him through that.

When she finally found the strength to end it for good she moved out of the home they had shared together and rented her own place. After a month or so he discovered her new address and started hounding her.

She had already had to change the number of her mobile phone because of his persistent phone calls, but when he started turning up outside her apartment at all hours, banging on the door and waiting outside her place of work, it all became too much.

She told us that she put all the energy and emotion she could muster into her Psychic Conversation and allowed herself to say all the things to him that she had been frightened to say before. Her desired outcome had been made very clear: she wanted him to leave her alone and was beyond the point of even hoping for any kind of apology.

Three days after her Psychic Conversation with her ex, she found a handwritten letter from him in her letterbox. Her first impulse was one of fear and to throw it away, imagining that it would contain more of the abuse and accusations that had become commonplace from him. To her relief and amazement, the letter was a long and emotional apology ending in a promise to never contact or try to find her again.

She had put the Psychic Conversation out of her mind and gotten on with her very busy life; she had a demanding job in I.T. and worked long hours. Like most people, she was also a little bit sceptical and didn't seriously expect much to happen. Having gone into the process with the attitude that it may help and wouldn't do any harm, she had not been sitting around waiting for something cataclysmic to happen.

As is so often the case when we just do our share of the 'work' and then let it go, the Universe had delivered something that far exceeded her expectations.

This lady continued to take part in the meditation classes for several months and stayed in contact as a private client, and I know she never heard from or saw this man again.

The technique of the Psychic Conversation is something that you can easily learn. Following the instructions above will get you started and that is really all you have to do.

Some people like to light a candle or call on their Angels to help them before starting, whatever works for you is just fine. As far as your conscious mind is concerned the Psychic Conversation will be taking place in your head, but when you put your positive intention behind it and your honest emotion and feeling into it, you will be communicating from your heart. The person on the receiving end may not like or agree with what you have to say, but when something is done with integrity and honesty then it cannot be denied.

Sometimes the outcome of a Psychic Conversation is simply to 'agree to disagree' and is an opportunity for your feelings to be aired even though the relationship is over. At other times however, it can facilitate the creation of very positive changes, stronger understanding and bonds.

So go ahead and enjoy yourself as you learn to use this process, and remember you can use the Psychic Conversation for 'good' things too. If someone in your life that you adore is a bit prickly and difficult to get close to, you can also use the Psychic Conversation to tell them that you love them.

FURTHER READING ON RELATED SUBJECTS:

The Power of Your Subconscious Mind by Dr. Joseph Murphy

CHAPTER 7

The art of automatic writing

'Having experienced several wonderful clairvoyant sessions with Belinda, I was beginning to open to the idea that perhaps indeed we all have a means of connecting with an unseen form of guidance that I now seem to "know" exists. I know it in the sense that I feel it in an unquestioning way . . . something that seems to be "fact" as if programmed into my cells to "know and understand" when the time was right in my life.'

PATRICIA W. M.

Automatic writing is one of the most effective ways to work with and strengthen your psychic connection. It is simply another form of channelling and one that really helps you to feel the difference between receiving your Divine Guidance as compared to your usual train of thought.

Recording the guidance that comes to you and through you is also an excellent way to capture the flow of information as it happens; becoming a permanent record for you to look over again whenever you want. It is very easy to forget what it is that you saw or said, or for other people to interpret it differently, but when you write something down, as it comes to you in the moment, it provides you with a wonderful record not just of the information you received but of your increasing clarity as you practice over time.

I still laugh when I look back on some of my old scribbling. When I started practicing automatic writing years ago I used to write down the strangest things. It would often start at around three o'clock in the morning after I had woken up from a dream or gone to the bathroom. As I was drifting back off to sleep one of my ears would start ringing, sometimes quite loudly so that I couldn't ignore it.

I soon learned that if I picked up my pen and paper and started writing that the ringing noise would go away. Back in those days I had an enormous bedroom and I had built a pyramid at one end of the room made out of copper piping. At the time I believed that sitting under this pyramid-shaped frame helped me to be more receptive to the incoming information, but when winter came I decided that I would just have to practice my automatic writing from the cosy warmth of my bed.

The words that flowed from my pen at that time made little if any sense. Here again I would like to remind you of the rusty pipes analogy. Much of what I wrote was the same sentence or idea repeated over and over again, nonsensical babbling that I could easily have ignored as rubbish and I was inclined to forget the whole thing.

I also received a great deal of 'information' in garbled French and Elizabethan style English, complete with all the 'thees and thys and thous'! Odd as this all seemed to me at the time, it didn't feel like a problem. I knew that my Guidance was contacting me at that early hour because that was when my mind was least cluttered with the thoughts and concerns of my everyday life. It was the easiest time for them to get through to me, when the activity of my conscious mind was at its lowest ebb.

It is a peculiar feeling at first, this business of automatic writing. We are so accustomed to our minds supposedly being in control of everything we do, so just letting go and allowing something to flow through you and onto the page is a challenge for some.

I believe that automatic writing has been around for a very long time; writers of poetry, prose and music throughout the ages speak of that urging of inspiration that simply can't be ignored and must be written down immediately without any censoring on their part.

Some of our greatest inventors and scientists have similar experiences. Dr. Samuel Hahnemann, the man who invented modern Homoeopathy was known to work and write throughout the night, as if driven by a force more powerful than himself, and often not sleeping for two days and nights in a row. He did this for many years, well into old age.

Many of the great composers, not only Mozart, are renowned for how incredibly young they were when they composed their miraculous music and for how quickly they wrote them.

Automatic writing is often a very quick process that does not allow the conscious mind time to analyse or criticise what is being written. You become a Channel for a stream of Divine Inspiration that completely bypasses your own knowledge base and thinking mind. You can always go back and correct it later if you like, but once your rusty water becomes a clear flow you probably won't need to.

When I was young I used to quite enjoy writing poetry, but the most beautiful poems I have ever written came to me decades later, at three or four in the morning, took less than five minutes to write and needed no correction of any kind. Here is one example:

~ THE WORLD WITHIN ~

She floats on mists of sand and sea
'Tween day and starry night,
Longing only to be free
Her sovereign, holy right.
The gold and silver of the dawn
Flows gently through her hair,
And such a scene of beauty born
Great things beyond compare.
Her heav'nly heart and earthly mind
Now shining with the Light,
With joy of life of different kind
Comes seeking from the night.
Perfection, neither here nor there
Resides the world within,
All that is good and fine and rare
Exists inside her skin.

Belinda and Friends

You may have noticed that I signed this poem 'Belinda and Friends'; I do this because I know that it wasn't myself alone who wrote it. I take the credit for developing my ability to write automatically to such a beautiful degree, for making myself available so to speak, but the actual content came from something greater than my conscious mind.

I call it the Universe, God/Goddess/All That Is or my Angels, Spirit Guides or Divine Guidance. It was inspiration (to be filled with Spirit/God) pure and simple, not something that my conscious mind had been working on. I had help of the most wonderful kind in writing it and I like to acknowledge that.

This poem, like all the others, came to me unexpectedly at what could be considered an inconvenient hour. It's wonderful to have these spontaneous bursts of creativity but that is only one of the forms of automatic writing.

The form that my students, clients and I use most of all is automatic writing on demand, an amazingly useful tool that can help you to receive excellent answers to your problems, be more creative or even write a book. In the following exercise you will find out how to get started, beyond that there are as many ways to use automatic writing as you can dream up.

Naturally I do recommend working with all the techniques in the previous chapters of this book first, as it is much easier to get clear information with a Channel that has already been set up for that purpose. It took me about four years to develop from the gobbledegook stages of my early scribblings to the clarity of the poem you have just read. I believe that one of the reasons it took me so long was that I was just muddling through it on my own.

Nowadays my students start practicing automatic writing in the fourth week of the courses I teach, often with stunning results, because their Channels have been reactivated and strengthened and they have learned how to connect to their Divine Guidance at will. If you have been using this book as instructed then you will have learned how to do this too and are now building on those important foundations.

Automatic writing is not about writing down what it is that you want to hear and then pretending that you Channelled it from a higher source, it is a genuine tool that allows you to access information from beyond the limited realm of human thinking, free of all the usual manipulations and underlying motives that come with most of our opinions and desires. So before starting the following exercise, give some thought to the kinds of questions you would like to ask.

It is always advisable to start with questions that don't hold a big emotional charge for you personally. For example if you were to ask a question such as 'Am I going to lose my job?' or 'Is my boyfriend going to ask me to marry him?' it is very difficult to remain impartial. Until you have a reasonable mastery of this tool it is best to steer clear of these kinds of enquiries because your impartiality is very important.

All the processes in this book are tools to help us surrender and allow ourselves to be guided by something greater than what we think we are.

The following list of questions will give you an idea of the kind of questions which are useful when just starting out. Many of them are questions I use in my classes.

- What is the meaning and/or purpose of rainbows?
- Is there life on other planets?
- What is the purpose of human suffering?
- What purpose do individuals such as Adolf Hitler serve in the process of human development?
- What do I need to understand or realise or embrace or let go of, in order to live a happier and more fulfilling life?

Try to notice the different feelings you have when Channelling an answer for a question you know absolutely nothing about, compared to one where you already have some opinions or beliefs. This will be a useful indicator for you as to what feels like an impartial Channel and what doesn't.

These are just a small sample of the questions you can start with. Choose one and then follow the steps of the following exercise to start your automatic writing practice. Allow your hand and pen to do the writing for you, without intervention from your mind. Remember there are no right or wrong answers, just be aware of your intention to be impartial and let the information flow.

EXERCISE TEN

AUTOMATIC WRITING – JUST DO IT!

REQUIREMENTS: a quiet location where you can sit and write comfortably

Notebook or Journal

Pen or Pencil

TIME REQUIRED: 10–30 minutes

(more than 30 minutes will give you writer's cramp!)

- Make yourself comfortable and remember to connect to the beam of white light that flows down through you from the Universe and into the core of the Earth, and the beam of red light that flows up to you from the Earth's core and up out through the top of your head.

- Sit with that energy flow for a moment until you feel 'plugged in' or connected.

Note: Eventually this connection will become instantaneous, activated by your intention to work with this, or one of the other techniques.

- Focus your intent on automatic writing and allowing yourself to become a Channel for information that you will write down.

- Let your conscious, thinking mind take a step back and do your best to accept that the information you are about to write down may not have anything to do with what you think, believe or have learned. Let this be a relaxing process, remain calm and alert while letting whatever information that wants to come to you flow in.

- Take up your pen and notebook, and focus on one question for a moment, all the while remaining aware of your intention. Write the chosen question at the top of the page first to help you get started.

Note: When you are new to this practice it is common to feel stuck or blocked at first, so be patient with yourself. Sometimes it's helpful to choose another question or to word it in a way that is more acceptable to you.

- Let your hand do the writing; let the words flow out onto the page however they come. This is not a test and we do not expect you to come up with eloquent or flowery verses at this early stage. Let it all happen without judgement or criticism, and please don't try to read it as you are writing it, that will certainly tempt you to analyse it and will block the flow.

- The only time to stop and read it is when you feel that you are completely finished with that question. If you would like to attempt more than one question on your first sitting then go right ahead, and notice the differences in the quality of the responses.

- Then practice, practice, practice whenever you can. Asking friends, friends-of-friends and family to give you simple questions can be helpful too, some of a more general nature, and eventually ones that are of a personal nature as well.

- Be sure to read your responses carefully and reflect on what they might be trying to tell you as well as taking the literal meanings.

Some of you may get incomprehensible or nonsensical 'stuff' like I did at first; others will get single words that make individual points rather than forming a sentence. At other times you may get a more steady flow only to find that it stops abruptly for no apparent reason. Just go with it and allow your skill to develop in its own natural way.

Keep practicing and expanding your repertoire. Once you have more confidence with this skill you can try answering questions that have an emotional charge. This will develop your ability to be impartial and make you into a more effective Channel. The more you are able to keep your own ideas and opinions out of it the more space you will leave for the Universe to work its magic.

It is also possible to use Automatic Writing as a way to get information and guidance for a friend, family member or client. However, when you are channelling information for another person there are responsibilities on both sides.

For the psychic it is very important that you make the other person aware of your level of experience, or lack thereof. Your other key responsibility is to hold an intention of wanting only the best for the other person by being the clearest Channel possible. This means being honest with yourself about whether or not your own opinions or judgements are colouring the information you are bringing through.

Be humble and let them know that perhaps some of your own ideas are in the mix of your channelled information.

The other responsibility lies with the receiver. The exact same piece of information will often be understood in 10 different ways by 10 different people as they filter it through their own experiences and beliefs. Be clear with those on the receiving end that how they interpret the information they are given, and how they choose to act upon it, is up to them, and totally their own responsibility.

Personally, when I first practiced in this way, I found it was best to know as little about the person as possible, so I preferred working with friends-of-friends, rather than my own. As I became more experienced I was able to channel impartial information for those familiar to me as well.

But no matter what your level of experience or who you are channelling for, it is possible to channel some wonderful information and creative work. Here is an example of some of the magical work that my students have achieved. Heather was a participant in one of my nine week courses; she is a scientist and had never done any work of this nature before. This is what she wrote in response to the question 'How can we connect more to the energies of the Goddess and bring more of the Goddess into our lives?'

~ THE GODDESS WITHIN ~

'You are all the Goddess

Connect with yourselves, your own inner beauty and love.

You are beautiful within and it should shine for all to see.

Trust in yourselves and know that you are all very special and beautiful people.

Love your life, your love and your inner self and laugh, laugh, laugh and be happy!

You are as special as everyone on this planet and you should show your inner Goddess to the world.

FURTHER READING ON THIS SUBJECT:

Opening to Channel by Sanaya Roman
How to do Automatic Writing by Edain McCoy

CHAPTER 8

Writing letters to your Angels

'My Dear Angels, I would like it very much if you could ask my son's Angels to take special care of him while he is on his travels. I know that as a mother I probably worry too much, but he does insist on going to some remote and even dangerous places. Would you all please keep an eye on him and make sure he is safe? Many thanks for that.
With gratitude as always.'

J. MARSH

While we are in a writing mood you may like to know that one of the easiest and most effective ways to communicate with your Angels is to write them a letter. Putting things down on paper is a marvellous way to focus your energy and attention.

When you first begin to meet your Angels and Spirit Guides it can be difficult to know how to stay in contact with them or to communicate with them about something specific or profound.

In the chapter on meeting your Angels and Spirit Guides I recommend that you speak to them in your mind or even out loud, and you should definitely do this on a daily basis to help your relationship with them grow. So when you wake up in the morning ask your Angels and Spirit Guides to gather around you and join you for the day.

However when it comes to something very specific or important to you, it might be worth taking the time to write it down. There is an energy or power to writing that goes beyond the thoughts that move around in your head. Writing it down sharpens the focus of those ideas and increases the intensity by turning something that is non-physical (thoughts) into something physical (the written word).

If you have a problem that continues to bother you the actual process of writing the letter can help you recognise some possible solutions even before you have sent it.

The best time to write a letter to your Angels or Spirit Guides is when you get a strong urge to do so, that is when you will put the greatest emotion and intensity into it. Don't feel that you have to hold back or be 'nice' either; you cannot offend your Angels or Spirit Guides, they have literally seen it all before. The main thing is to be genuine about your desire for a solution or the item or situation you want.

Sometimes we believe that our prayers or requests go unanswered, but the truth is we only get what we *really* want. Even if we have convinced ourselves that we want a certain thing at the level of the logical mind, we will not receive it if it is clear that our hearts yearn for something else. Remember, the Universe doesn't speak any particular language, what it responds to is our feelings about life and ourselves.

Over the years my clients, students and I have had some delightful and interesting responses to our letters. One recent example was really quite amazing.

Charlotte was a student of mine and had a very important job in an insurance firm. With all her knowledge and experience it should have been a rewarding and even enjoyable role, but her time with this company was fraught with difficulties from day one. Her biggest problem was the total lack of respect with which some of her junior staff treated her. They spoke to her rudely and a couple of them even openly defied her and refused to do as she directed even though they were fully aware that she was their supervisor.

After three months of this Charlotte went home one evening after work feeling completely exasperated. Frustrated and angry about what was going on, she wrote a very passionate letter to her Angels. She addressed it to them by name and did not hold back on her true feelings about these people, their rudeness, and her own hurt, embarrassment and confusion. All her years of training and experience in this field had not prepared her for such insubordination and she had no idea what to do; it all came pouring out onto the page, which in itself was a cathartic process.

When she asked her Angels how to send this letter to them she was answered by a strong feeling to take the letter out into the garden and burn it. She also asked them to give her a sign that they had received the letter. By this time it was late so she burned the letter at the bottom of the garden and went to bed.

The next day she left for work and as she opened the gate she noticed a large feather stuck on the top of it. This had never happened before and she felt very strongly that it was the sign from her Angels to signify the receipt of her letter.

Once at work the following few hours were quite amazing, as each of the four people who had been so uncooperative up to this time made contact with her by email or phone. One of them rang her and actually apologised for his behaviour, another called and asked her advice on a certain project and listened attentively to her advice. The other two people were suddenly friendly and professional in their approach.

Charlotte was pleasantly stunned at the transformations; she had not spoken to any of them directly, the only thing that had changed since the day before was that she had written the letter to her Angels. Now all the people involved were being nice to her.

At this point you could be forgiven for thinking that this is the end of the story, but a few days later two more feathers crossed her path in very unusual places. She had a distinct feeling that something major was going to happen later that day, didn't know what it was going to be, but felt that the feathers were her Angels' way of letting her know that they were near and that everything would be okay.

At lunchtime she was summoned to the top floor to see her manager, this was not a scheduled meeting and they would not tell her what it was about over the phone. Once she got to his office he promptly sat her down and told her that her employment contract was being terminated, her probationary period still had a few days to run, there was nothing she could do or say, it was over, and she left the company that day for good.

Naturally she was upset at first and felt that she had been unfairly treated, then it dawned on her what was really going on. When she was totally honest with herself she had to admit that she had hated that job from the first day, and that the only thing that had kept her there was the fear of change and the loss of her good salary. She didn't think it would look good on her CV to leave that job too soon and chose to stick with the 'rational' path of putting up with it.

But Charlotte had triggered a big energy shift by writing that letter. Not only did the Angels show her that they could help with the superficial problem of the difficult people, they also responded to the true desire expressed by her which was 'I hate my job but I cannot logically justify leaving it at this time. Help!' By losing her job Charlotte actually got what she really wanted.

We all try to talk ourselves into doing what seems right or safe, most people do it for their entire lives, seeing anything else as an unjustifiable risk and fearing the criticism of others. Charlotte's

Angels helped her to see the bigger picture of what was really going on in her life and helped her to acknowledge that she has been longing for a career change for years. Suddenly her situation took on a different complexion and instead of fearing life without her job she realised how many other opportunities she had. So caught up in the idea that she had to be self-sufficient, she hadn't even realised that her husband was willing to support her while she explored new career and study options. Sure, they might have to watch their spending a little for a while, but they would get by and everything would be alright. The Universe responded to her true desire and she was catapulted into the next phase of her life.

This is just one example of the ways in which your help will come. Often our minds are quite fixed on *the way things should happen* and we miss the gifts that come our way because they don't look like we expected them to. The nasty, uncooperative people whom Charlotte had to supervise were actually the Universe's way of telling her that she no longer belonged in that kind of environment. When she didn't take the hint and cried out for help that good old Cosmic Boot came along again to give her a nudge in a much healthier direction.

This is powerful stuff we are working with here, it transforms people's lives every day. So be honest with yourself about what you *really* want and be prepared for it to come to you in unusual ways. Charlotte could have wallowed in the idea of her termination as a disaster and remained angry and hurt for any length of time. What she decided to do instead was to see it as a gift and the chance to start a whole new career path. She is happily doing that as I write these words and not missing her old corporate life. Oh, and by the way, a few weeks after this big life change her husband received a huge pay rise.

EXERCISE ELEVEN

WRITING A LETTER TO YOUR ANGELS OR SPIRIT GUIDES

REQUIREMENTS: a quiet location where you can sit and write comfortably

Writing paper

Envelope

Pen or pencil

OPTIONAL: Candles

Music

Oil burner with some nice essential oil of your choice

Postage stamps

TIME REQUIRED: 10–30 minutes

- Start by tuning yourself in to the energy flow through your Channel to create your connection to your Divine Guidance and ask your Angels and Spirit Guides to gather around you.
- Set a nice mood if you like by lighting a candle and putting on some relaxing music.
- Be as clear as you can about what it is you want and write it all down on your writing paper.
- If you don't know the names of your Angels and Spirit Guides yet then simply address it to 'My Dear Angels' or something like that.

- Write the letter as you would to a friend who knows you very well and wants to help you. Your Angels and Spirit Guides are not hung up on formalities, so make it as friendly and direct as you want.

Note: Don't leave anything out because of some mistaken belief that you can overload them or ask too much. Your celestial friends can deal with anything you can dish up.

- Once you have finished writing, put your letter in an envelope and address it to them.

Note: you can even put a stamp on it to make it feel more authentic!

- Ask your Angels or Spirit Guides how they would like you to send it and go with the first impulse that comes to you, whether it be burying it, burning it, casting it out onto the ocean, tearing it up into tiny pieces, putting it in a drawer or even in the recycling. I have put some of my letters in the post.

- As you 'send' your letter ask your Angels or Guides for a sign to let you know it has been received.

- Once you have completed and sent the letter do not dwell on the situation or the possible solution, trust that all that can be done is being done by your Angels and wait for the results to manifest for you without anxiety.

VALIDATION

The signs that your letter has been received by your friends are as varied as they are. Some of you might notice a feather in an unusual place, or the words of a song you have heard a hundred times may suddenly strike you as important.

When I ask for a sign of acknowledgement I am often shown a rainbow in the most peculiar of places, maybe one in the sky even when there hasn't been any rain, or in the colours of someone's clothing or a rainbow lorikeet flying onto my windowsill.

The signs are often very subtle and you may miss them at first. The main thing is that with your strong and clear intention to get a message to your Angels and/or Spirit Guides you can be sure that it has been done. Being given a sign is really just a reassurance for the mind. Once you have 'sent' the letter your only job is to let go of the problem and let the solutions come by being open to them appearing in ways you had not anticipated. This is not the Universe trying to test you, it is just trying to give you the best possible result and usually one that will exceed your expectations.

Most of all this process should be done in a spirit of fun. Even when your problems are serious or your situation is dire your Angels and Spirit Guides will often bring a solution to you that is humorous or lighthearted, this is not flippancy but rather an acknowledgement that we can achieve a lot more when we are joyous and relaxed as opposed to squeezing the life force out of it with grim determination.

Write your letter, send it and then relax. You will be prompted to take the next step when it is required.

The only thing you need to practice with this technique is your ability to recognise and respond to the prompts and signs. This ability will develop with practice, so write lots of letters in order to give yourself plenty of opportunities to improve.

A few years ago I had a response from my Angels that took my breath away. It was the middle of winter and I had a very strong urge to write a letter to my Angels, so I sat down and wrote with great passion and detail.

When I was finished they told me very clearly to go and cast my letter out onto the ocean. I live minutes from the beach so this was easy enough, but they were very specific as they told me it had to be on the next high tide which was at 10 o'clock that night!

The wind and waves were wild that evening as it had been stormy for days, but I rugged up and went out as instructed. After two attempts at flinging my envelope out into the crashing waves I was becoming cold, wet and a little exasperated. I told myself that if the third throw was no good I was going to take my letter and go home. The third attempt was good of course, and my letter got sucked out into the night.

The following day I tried to go for a walk on the beach three or four times but every time I went to walk out of the building the rain lashed down and I went back inside. Finally at around three o'clock it looked fine enough to go out. The tide was very low and the expanse of flat, glassy sand shone in the wintry sun. As I passed the spot on the beach where I had stood the night before, I began to wonder if I was going to get a sign.

As I continued to walk I noticed some writing in the sand a couple of hundred metres further along. Tourists and children were always writing messages in the sand, usually along the lines of 'Johnny loves Jane' or 'I was here' and things like that. The first noticeably different things about this message was that it was very long and written so neatly it was as though it had been meticulously measured out, the lettering also looked very fresh, as though they had only just been written but there was no one nearby. It was the words however, that both stunned me and made me laugh; they read: 'Wednesday 10th of May. We hope you have had a nice day. We look forward to reading your letter.'

After reading that message in the sand there was certainly no doubt that my Angels had received my letter.

FURTHER READING ON THIS SUBJECT:

Angelspeake: How to Talk With Your Angels by Barbara Mark
Spirit Guides and Angel Guardians: Contact Your Invisible Helpers by Richard Webster

CHAPTER 9

Breaking the cycle – releasing your past life patterns

'It had been a year since my last visit to Belinda, and I knew that it was the right time to go back. My husband and I desperately wanted a baby, but we had no luck becoming pregnant. During my past life reading it was revealed to me that events from one of my lifetimes hundreds of years ago had left me with deep feelings of sexual guilt and shame. It was a huge relief to bring these feelings into the open and let them go. Less than one month later I fell pregnant, and now have a beautiful baby girl.'

CAITLIN

The phrase 'you can't take it with you' is only partially right. You may not be able to take your favourite shoes or your bank balance with you when you pass over, but unresolved emotional issues will stay with you until you deal with them. Your soul will keep attracting the same kinds of people and circumstances to you, life after life after life, until you get it. This may seem cruel to some but it is just the working of a very orderly Universe which demonstrates that every action, be it a feeling, belief, thought, word or deed (yes, all of those things are actions) has an effect.

By examining your past lives, and resolving the negative patterns or issues that you still carry from those times, you can create positive changes in your current life. Hearing about a past life may be a curiosity or entertainment for some, but for me and my clients it has become a path to greater understanding of the self and the freedom that brings. So it's not about dwelling on the past at all, it's about making the present more pleasant.

Once a young woman came to see me for a reading. She was on crutches, with her right foot heavily bandaged. I soon discovered that she was only 24, and that, despite all kinds of examinations by specialists, including X-rays, no cause for her problem had been found. Finally, in an attempt to give it some sort of label, she had been diagnosed with gout, which seemed quite unlikely given her youth and healthy lifestyle. She was in excruciating pain, moving or touching the foot was impossible, but she did not want to take the steroids she had been prescribed.

This was the first time I had been asked to work on someone with acute physical pain, but I did what I always do and closed my eyes and waited for the guidance and information to come.

What followed in the reading was the tale of Claudia, a detailed description of one of my young client's past lives where she was a foreign gypsy girl with a flair for herbal medicine.

Claudia's story revealed

FRANCE 17TH CENTURY

It would be fair to say that Claudia was an enigma to most of the folk in her large French town. She was a strange looking creature to most peoples' eyes for she had the pale skin of someone from the north, and the thick, dark, wavy hair of a Mediterranean woman. Her appearance was somewhat unkempt, and her dress sense would often cause the people that she met to believe that she was a gypsy.

Some of the town's people liked her, some were curious, but most found her distasteful and avoided her.

However Claudia had great skill with medicinal herbs and, exasperated by the lack of results that they had from their physicians, or unable to afford one, some townsfolk sought her out as a last resort. Although they were often grateful for her vast and eclectic body of knowledge most still found it prudent not to acknowledge her openly in public.

Claudia was not concerned with her herbal healing arts on this particular night however, because the person she was going to visit was already beyond that kind of help. He was a boy who had died at the age of 15 after being flogged by his master for theft. The master would not allow the boy to have any medical attention, and when the boy died he had him cheaply and hastily buried in the town cemetery. No one else attended and no one seemed to care, except Claudia.

Now, having waited till it was late and all was quiet, she crept into the cemetery in order to sing some prayers over the fresh grave and place some petals and herbs upon it, to help hasten and ease the passage of the young man's soul.

As she sang and spoke to him, and placed some flower petals and other simple items in a particular pattern on the earth, she heard voices coming closer through the darkness. She hoped that they would pass, but it seemed that they were coming directly into the cemetery.

The last thing she wanted was to be discovered there by people who were already somewhat suspicious of her behaviour, she did not want to be imprisoned or ejected from the town, as had happened to other misfits in the past.

Claudia knew there was only one entrance to the grounds which would lead her towards the voices. Unwilling to risk being caught, she ran instead towards the perimeter fence and began to scramble over it.

The fence was a tall, wrought iron affair with large spikes along the top, it was dangerous to climb but she wasn't thinking clearly and just wanted to get out. She pulled herself to the top and brought her right foot over, lost her balance momentarily and impaled her right foot on one of the huge spikes. Frantic now, Claudia managed to pull her foot back up off the spike and scramble down the other side of the fence.

Claudia did not dare to go out into the streets for several days and felt fortunate that she could at least tend to her wound properly.

A week later hunger forced her to go out to the market for food, but no one paid her any mind and her life soon returned to normal, never being questioned about her whereabouts that night. She listened for any gossip on the street but heard none.

Claudia remained in that town for many years helping those who came to her with their ailments and still performing the occasional ceremony over the graves of the uncelebrated people of the town. It was her fate also to remain an unsung member of her community, despite helping so many for little or even no remuneration.

At the end of her life she was given a paupers grave and was forgotten. Most would have described her life as unimportant, but Claudia felt differently. She had enjoyed her work, her freedom and her independence so much that even though she was nearly 70 when she died she felt that she wanted to continue to be here in the world. People needed her and here is where she wanted to stay. So her soul remained connected to the Earth plane.

After the reading my client told me that she was a Naturopathy student and dreamed of having her own practice one day as a healer. She loved learning about all the remedies and herbs, and we could see from her life as Claudia that she was already well prepared for this kind of career path.

A week later she came back to see me, walking very well without her crutches, but the pain in her foot was not entirely gone. We did a bit more clearing work and asked her Angels to make sure that that aspect of her soul had gone completely to the Light. As always, everything that needed to be done was taken care of and all of her attachment to that past life was released. The pain in her foot cleared up completely within the next week and has never troubled her again.

A graphic illustration indeed of how the energy from an unresolved past life can come back to affect you in the present, and just one example of the good things that can happen for us when we learn how to liberate ourselves from our past.

Some of the experiences that you had in your previous incarnations still play a part in the way you feel and behave today. When you came into this current lifetime your soul decided to have certain types of experiences for many different reasons. All of them will ultimately lead to greater spiritual growth and awareness, what we sometimes refer to as enlightenment, and they broadly fall in to three large categories: *Experiences, People* and of course, *Past Life Issues*.

The new *Experiences* such as living in a country that you never have before, or anything that you have not yet done in a previous life, are designed to help you to expand your sense of who you are.

Then there are the Experiences that are similar to the things you enjoyed or were good at in the past and want more time to refine. You may be drawn to a certain hobby or vocation with a power that you can't explain, perhaps even finding that you are a 'natural' at this activity.

It is equally possible to be drawn to certain *People* with whom you immediately feel a positive bond, instinctively you feel that you have been friends before, but in the absence of 'proof' most people let that notion go.

The third category, *Past Life Issues*, is much less amusing. This consists of all the experiences which bring you reminders of the feelings, beliefs, thoughts, words and actions that caused you some kind of pain, misfortune or confusion in your past life or lives. It will also encompass all the things about yourself that you don't like, your negative beliefs and expectations, and the things you wouldn't or seemingly couldn't deal with and resolve at an earlier time.

Even after hundreds of lives, there are still many new and pleasant experiences available to us, but most of us will also have a closet full of baggage that is dragging us down.

Most of the lives that will be shown to you are the ones that hold something you have not yet understood or come to terms with, and only you can know what those things are. You are the only person qualified to intrepret the meaning of what you are shown.

When a person comes to me for a reading I usually ask them only for the most mundane of information: name, date of birth, address, phone numbers, yet after the reading they report to me how amazed they are by the similarities between the past life that came up to be cleared and what they are experiencing now.

Most of us have had hundreds of lives here on Earth, some of which may have only lasted a few minutes or hours, as infant mortality was extremely high in bygone centuries. No matter how brief though, it still counts as a life, and although it may seem tragic to those who are left behind, the soul of each human being knows exactly when it is the right time to depart.

The Angels have always told me and my clients that there is no such thing as an untimely, premature or accidental death and that each soul has a contract to incarnate here on Earth for specific reasons, experiences and periods of time. This is not a haphazard Universe, everything happens for a reason even if we find it difficult to accept. Your soul will remain in this incarnation for exactly the amount of time that it needs to in order to experience what it came here for.

Ultimately once you get to the point where you have lived many lives, and connect with some of your memories of them, you begin to have compassion for and understanding of people from other cultures and walks of life. As you realise that you have walked in many different kinds of shoes.

Many clients of mine are amazed to find that they have been both victim and villain in the great story of humanity. We all love to hear stories of how hard we tried, how good we were and how unfairly we were treated, but it is also very humbling to know that at some point we were all criminals, liars, cheats and even murderers.

Those of you who are women in this life have lived here before as men, and vice versa, so it is no good pointing the finger anymore and trying to blame some other group or gender for 'the mess we are in.' We have all been greedy and we have all been generous, a fact that is vital to understand if the wounds of humanity are ever to be fully healed. Discovering that you have been many different kinds of people in the past is a process of self-forgiveness and an act of courage, for none of us are superior to another in the end.

The past life reading and healing process that my Angels taught me is very thorough. It is a process that goes much deeper than just telling a story. Over the years I have had many people come to me and tell me that another reader had told them that they had had a past life in a certain place, doing this or that. A snippet of the story was thrown their way but nothing more. No detail about the experiences of that life, the lessons that went unlearned or whether or not there were unresolved issues remaining.

In our process you will be able to discover not only as much detail about your past life story as you can, you will also be taught how to resolve the issues from that life and move on. It is a complete process which will leave you with a greater understanding of who you are and the journey you are on.

If you keep making the same mistakes, coming up against similar obstacles and frustrations, find yourself dealing with the same kind of difficult people over and over again, then clearing past life patterns may help you.

Whether a hurt went unaddressed a week ago, a year ago, a lifetime ago or centuries ago is of no consequence, the fact is that it still needs to be healed. Past life review and release will help you clear these kind of pains, and the patterns and problems they cause, forever.

EXERCISE TWELVE

PAST LIFE RELEASE

In this simple, step-by-step exercise you will review and release one of your own past lives. Please read the guidelines in full a couple of times before doing the exercise. At first glance you may think that there is a lot to remember, but it really is very simple and has a logical, step by step flow.

REQUIREMENTS: a quiet location where you can lie or sit comfortably

Pen

Notebook or Journal

TIME REQUIRED: Approx. 30 minutes

- Have a pen and notepad or journal within arms reach of where you will sit.

- Make yourself comfortable, close your eyes and ask your Angels and Spirit Guides to come and gather closely around you. Tune in to your intention to review and release one of your own past lives. If you are feeling particularly troubled by a certain issue at this time, you may want to ask your Angels and Spirit Guides to help you see the past life in which the root cause of that issue was created, or you may be happy to go with the flow and review whatever life comes up.

- Imagine all the colours of the rainbow – red, orange, yellow, green, blue, indigo and violet – and picture those colours on your Inner Screen. Contemplate them for a minute or so then allow yourself to be drawn into one of those colours.

- Allow yourself to be drawn in deeply, as though the colour is engulfing you or you are diving into it, gently reminding yourself of your intention to revisit one of your own past lives. You may feel like you are travelling through a tunnel of this colour, or imagine you are swimming or floating through it. Take as long as you like on this colourful journey, there is no rush.

- Gently direct yourself to emerge from the colour into the environment of your past life. Give yourself time to get a sense of having arrived, start by focusing on your feet or some other part of your body or appearance, such as clothing. Allow the story to unfold on your Inner Screen in your mind's eye. Don't 'try' to see anything, just let it happen. Allow your mind to go blank so that your past life story can come to you, like the return of a very old memory.

- The story may come to you fleetingly, as a feeling or unconnected images or sounds. Stay with it, relax and don't try to analyse or understand it yet. In your mind, ask questions about the things that you would like to know, such as are you male or female? What country are you in? What century or year is it? What sort of family did you have? What did you do with your time? Did you get an education, work, get married? And so on.

- Try to imagine that you are watching a movie of your past life playing in your head. You have the remote control, so rewind it to the beginning and direct it to play in chronological order from start to finish.

- Stay with the experience until you feel that you have been shown everything that you were meant to see. Coax as much detail out of it as you can and continue to nudge the information along until you sense that you are coming to the end of that life story. Most people are curious to know how old they were when they died and what they died from, so ask about these things too if they interest you.

- Before you leave ask why you were shown this particular past life and why it is still not fully resolved; why did this aspect of your soul not go to the Light?

Note: There could be many reasons including deeply held religious beliefs in that life, or loved ones who you didn't want to be separated from, or a desire you didn't get to realise.

- When you have done your best to get a sense of the answers to these questions call your Angels and Spirit Guides in to assist that aspect of yourself on its journey up to the Light. Imagine all the heaviness and unhappiness from that lifetime being absorbed by the Light, that part of your soul being compassionately embraced and welcomed without question, and experience the relief that comes.

- The next step is simply to let all the beautiful, positive energy, memories and personality traits from that life be returned to you in full. Picture a stream of golden energy flowing back down to you and pouring into your heart, returning to you all that was good and desirable from that life. These qualities will be reintegrated into your being in a way that is compatible and useful in this lifetime.

- Then, when you are ready, you can begin the return trip to your present place and time. Use the same colour that helped to transport you to the past life. (If your colour changes that is also perfectly fine.) Moving back along through your colourful superhighway, you have a calm sense of knowing that you are returning to your present life. Imagine yourself homing in on the country you live in, then the state, then the city, then the street, then the building, and so on, all the way back to the room you are in and the chair you are sitting on.

- Take a moment or two, eyes still closed, to become fully aware of your physical body again. Breathe deeply, feel the weight of your body in the chair, wriggle your fingers and toes and have a stretch if you like. Say your name out loud, for example 'I am BelindaGrace', then open your eyes.

- Before doing anything else, take up your pen and paper and write down all that you can remember about your experience. It is very important to do this right away because your memory of this journey can fade, just like the memory of a dream. Jot down details including any feelings or emotions that you had during the review.

- This final step is almost the most important. It's the step where I say to you – 'Don't worry! There is no wrong way to do this, you did it your way and you did it well. You read the guidelines and then you let it happen, and that is always the best way.' The most important step in all of these techniques is your intention, everything else will be done for you by your Angels and Spirit Guides whether you 'see' it or not.

A past life revealed

We have all had many positive and beautiful experiences in our pasts, these nice memories however are not usually the ones that need to be come to terms with and resolved. The happy memories are much more easily accepted and integrated, whereas the hurts and pains of everyday life are not. I believe that one of the main reasons that our painful experiences go unresolved is because deep down we always blame ourselves for them.

Even if we are outwardly blaming others for our problems, inside a little voice is saying 'What's wrong with me, why is this happening to me, why can't I get it right?' It is the lack of forgiveness that we afford ourselves that stops us from going to the Light, we feel undeserving of the unconditional love that is offered to us at the end of each incarnation, so we hold on to the negative feelings, hoping they will just disappear with time.

One of the key causes of depression that I have come across is a past life experience that was so traumatic for the individual that they lost their will to live. These traumatic experiences can range from the downright harrowing to a mild shock or fright, it all depends on the individual and the impact it had on them at the time.

One young woman who came to see me seemed to have everything to live for. She did her best to appear cheerful and positive while she was around other people, but at home by herself it was a very different story.

She felt suicidal and cried herself to sleep almost every night. She had kept these low feelings mostly to herself because she found that when she tried to talk to people about how badly she felt they seemed unable to understand or take her seriously. All they saw was a pretty, successful and likeable young woman with a good job and a loving fiancé. They couldn't really relate to the fact that inside she was miserable. She didn't understand it either and she felt foolish, almost disbelieving her own feelings because she always felt better around other people.

Her fiancé had talked to her about setting a wedding date and they were to marry six months from her first visit to me. They did not yet live together and she was dreading the whole thing because she knew she would not be able to repress her sad and frightened feelings every night after they were married. This lovely lady had not told her fiancé about her 'problem' and the counselling she had done had not been able to uncover the source of her seemingly inexplicable unhappiness.

We commenced the reading as always and I was shown a past life of hers which would be enough to turn anyone's hair grey.

During a lifetime in London in the early to mid 1800S she had been stalked and eventually kidnapped by a mentally deranged uncle. Her family were working class and she received a basic education, able only to read and write a little. They lived in the north east of London in the area of Finchley. In order to help the family supplement its income, at the age of 12 she went to work two or three days a week as a kind of trainee governess or nanny. It was a large household, the man of the house a very successful barrister with a sickly wife and six children. There was plenty of work to do and she enjoyed it, walking to and from her employer's home at the same time each day.

Meanwhile, her father's brother was being welcomed back into the family fold after a falling out many years earlier. She had not really had a chance to get to know him as he had been absent from the family since she was four or five.

During the reading it was unclear what the problem had been between her uncle and her father, but there was a strong sense that he had been in prison for some time for reasons no one seemed inclined to discuss.

Relations with her uncle and her family were on the mend and everyone seemed happy enough, and she continued to go to work at the barrister's home and was soon offered full-time employment there, much to the joy of everyone.

Her uncle, who now visited the family fairly often, would come and meet her in the evenings outside her employer's front gate, and walk her home. She understood that he was trying to be friendly, but there was something about him that made her feel uncomfortable. His behaviour towards her became overly familiar, encroaching on her physical space, touching her hair and being somewhat possessive of her when other people were around. He became angry when she hinted that she would rather walk home on her own, and he would sometimes insist that they walk much longer distances than were necessary to get back to her family.

One night, when his behaviour was quite unreasonable, she tried to run away from him. He had demanded that they walk through a large park together, it was cold and nearly dark and she felt afraid. She fled, but he caught up with her easily and, even though she struggled, he dragged her across the park and into a dilapidated building. It turned out to be a kind of squat very near to the grimy bed-sit where her uncle lived.

He tied her up and kept her there for days, even joining in the frantic search for her with her distraught family, saying that she had not been waiting as usual when he had gone to collect her the previous day.

On the seventh day of her ordeal she died of dehydration, terrified, alone and only a few miles from where she lived. Her uncle had been very clever, living in a small bed-sit just a block or two away, but spending most of his time at the squat, so when the police searched his home – the bed-sit – they found no sign of his niece.

He buried her beneath the floorboards and her body was never found.

The reasons for this man's behaviour and mental state are too complicated to go into here. What was made clear to us however was that the trauma of this experience had frightened her so much that she had lost her will to live. That aspect of her soul did not go to the Light when she died because she was so terrified and disorientated and wanted only to return to her parents.

Once we had heard the whole story her Angels came and helped that aspect of her soul go to the Light to find peace once and for all.

When an aspect of your soul that has been in limbo since the end of a particular life finally goes to the Light, miraculous things happen.

All the heaviness and negativity from that lifetime are allowed to fall away; any negative emotions or memories connected with that life are absorbed into the Light and embraced in a compassionate way.

This is a deeply healing process because a part of you that has been frightened and in pain for a long time is finally going home and experiencing the all-encompassing and unconditional love of the Creator. All positive memories, qualities and feelings from that lifetime are then returned to you and reintegrated into your awareness in a way that is useful for you in this lifetime. You are reunited with a part of yourself that has always been there but was disconnected from you until now.

The changes in this young woman's life were remarkable. She became her true self again: happy, positive and calm. She began to look forward to her wedding and the life she and her fiancé would build. The fears that had plagued her seemed to evaporate and the feelings of confusion and desperation went away. Now, years later, she is happily married and expecting her second child.

My experience revealed

Of course the best way to learn is to experience the process, so several years ago I decided that I wanted to investigate something from my own life. From the age of 12 I had always been adamant that I would never get married or have children, and used to voice these opinions with great conviction.

So, not surprisingly I found myself, at the age of 37, without a partner, not unhappy, but feeling that something wasn't right and that there was an emotional blockage for me somewhere in my history.

I used the exact same process outlined in this book, and held the intention that if there was a past life connected with my aversion to being married then I wanted to see it and clear it once and for all. My intention was clear and strong and what I saw was profound and amazing.

I found myself in the deep south of America; it was the mid 1800s, not long before the American Civil War. I was a dark-haired southern belle, from a very wealthy family.

My life was unusual in the sense that I was very well educated. My father was a man ahead of his time and saw no reason why his daughter should not be as well educated as his sons. I expressed a strong wish to study and perhaps even pursue a career in the law, as I was passionate about civil rights and social equality. My parents took all of this in their stride and they supported me in most of my endeavours.

At the age of 19 or 20 I met a man who would succeed in convincing me to marry him. Not only was he charming and handsome and from a good family, he was also a social activist and fought openly for the freedom of the Negro slaves and better living standards for the large numbers of poor people in our community. After nearly two years of fervent proposals he managed to convince me that I could still have all the freedom I wanted and pursue the things I was interested in as his wife. He made it clear that he would encourage and be proud of me and promised that we could work together, so I married him and believed I would be happy.

What I hadn't given much thought to before marrying him was the effect that having children would have on my life. I became pregnant in our first year together and another four children followed in quick succession. The hormonal highs and lows of five children in five years caused all the other hopes and dreams I had for my life to be thrown to the wind.

I was exhausted and often depressed, plus other problems were brewing on the horizon as well. My husband was becoming increasingly unpopular amongst his wealthy friends and business associates for his unorthodox views and outspoken manner. He was making enemies, his family had all but disowned him and our financial situation began to deteriorate rapidly.

One night, when my husband was out at a town meeting, I heard shouting and noises coming towards our house. Our home was pretty grand by normal standards, with a long gravel driveway coming up through the garden to the front of the house.

My children and I converged on the front verandah to see men with torches aflame, staggering, hollering and dragging something behind them. I began to shake, knowing something terrible had happened and I clutched onto my children as one of the men finally came forward from the mob. He announced that my husband had finally got what he deserved for supporting the Black people and making a mockery of all that the wealthy, white society had created and stood for.

This dreadful man yelled in this way for a minute or so and then beckoned to some others behind him. My husband's broken and battered body was dragged forward by these men and dumped right in front of us. He was dead; murdered by an angry mob of men who had felt threatened by him.

In that moment my life was completely destroyed. I was now a widow with five children to support, and no real income. I was distraught, frightened and broke.

It became clear to me as to why in this life I had been so adamant from a young age never to marry or have children.

With my Angel's help I sent this life to the Light and let all the pain from that experience go. As always, the positive qualities I had and positive memories and traits were all returned to me and reintegrated. It was a very powerful and enlightening process. Three weeks later I met a man who I married after a year, and there is no doubt in my mind that the understanding and resolution I gained from reviewing and releasing that past life cleared the way for this next important step in my life.

Over the years I have seen many people experience dramatic changes within themselves and their lives after having a past life reading with me or from doing the process for themselves.

Physical ailments have dramatically improved, relationships turned around and deep emotional and psychological traumas have been healed, so much so that I could write a book on these cases alone. Many of the people who come to me do so because they feel lost, confused, directionless or depressed. Helping them to relieve themselves of emotional baggage that has been with them for lifetimes gives them a fresh outlook and renewed energy to embrace life.

One of the most rewarding outcomes is that when we have finished dredging through the difficult and unpleasant stuff we begin to encounter past lives where there was a lot of happiness, success and so on. Once the shadows are gone from the cupboard then all the positives can be reintegrated as well.

FURTHER READING ON THIS SUBJECT:

Many Lives Many Masters by Dr. Brian Weiss
Life between Life by Dr. Joel Whitton and Joe Fisher

CHAPTER 10

Parallel lives

> *'It is the commonest of mistakes to consider that the limit of our power of perception is also the limit of all there is to perceive.'*
> *Man, Visible and Invisible*

C. W. LEADBEATER

The concept of concurrent or parallel lifetimes has long been explored by writers of science fiction and fantasy but there is a lot more to this than a good story. Eighty years ago quantum physicists discovered that photons and electrons can exist in more than one location at a time – which means that we can, and many of us do, live in more than one reality at a time.

Some people will experience their parallel life through a dream, others will see a flash of themselves in another place and time and some people simply live with a sense of knowing that the life they are now living here on Earth is not the only life they are in.

For the majority of people a parallel life can remain undiscovered, but every now and then one of my clients will be informed about their parallel life during a reading with me.

You might be thinking to yourself 'I have enough going on in this lifetime! Why do I need to know about another lifetime I am supposedly involved in somewhere else?' That's a good question, and one I can only answer through the responses of my clients and my own experiences with my concurrent life.

My own experiences with parallel life started around mid-2012 while I was dating a man who lived in the region of Australia I had recently moved to. We were drawn to each other instantly, despite our 17-year age difference and found that we had a great deal in common. One night, about three months into our relationship I was taken into my parallel life.

During my 'visit' I experienced myself as this other Being, a delightful young Soul who lived in an enormous forest full of trees so large that their bases were broader than a house. It was clear that I was very happy and my role was something like a herald as I moved around this forest-world from community to community delivering messages, bringing and sharing information and checking in for the latest news with each group.

Each time I reached a community or clan I was warmly greeted and made very welcome.

The Beings in this world all lived wholly with and from Nature, yet there was no sense of hardships, struggles with the elements or agricultural labour. In fact there was no agriculture at all to speak of, and, while everyone looked healthy, the only thing I saw anyone eat was forms of fungi and lichen. We also drank a brew that was non-alcoholic and similar to what I now know as kombucha (I had never heard of kombucha at the time of this experience).

Each community had a central area where meetings were held, surrounded of course by these glorious trees. We all sat in a circle and exchanged news, updates, ideas and greetings. I felt very safe and at home, no matter which community I visited. I didn't seem to live in any one particular place, yet always had a home wherever I was.

Then I was escorted through the trees to a beautiful grove where a man stood waiting to welcome me, to my astonishment it was my boyfriend! In this concurrent lifetime he was the leader or the elder of this particular community and I was the young messenger. As we spoke he led me towards a tree that was large by Earthly standards, but small compared to those that surrounded the grove and filled the forest. As we stood in front of this tree he gestured towards it, indicating that I should look at the broader, flatter side of the trunk that we now stood in front of.

Intrigued, I regarded the side of the tree as he had bid me to do, and gradually amazing patterns, similar to hieroglyphics or runes, began to appear in the bark. We stood reading the symbols for some minutes and he had to explain the significance of some of them to me. I felt that I was stepping up to a new level of qualification as a messenger and that this leader was teaching me the language of these symbols and how to stimulate their appearance on certain, special trees.

Eventually the symbols faded again and he bid me farewell. It was such an unusual experience because at the same time I could feel my utter surprise as BelindaGrace observing these events and could feel myself as this other, forest-dwelling Being, taking it all in my stride, perfectly happy and just getting on with my day.

Unable to contain my excitement I woke up and immediately woke my boyfriend. We discussed the whole experience at length and to my further astonishment he found that it totally resonated with him!

Over the next few days we made deliberate attempts to glean more information from this concurrent world and my boyfriend received some fleeting impressions and flickering glimpses. He didn't fully trust these messages because of what I had already told him, but we persevered. I, however, was able to understand so much more.

The sensation for me was like stepping through an opening that was gauzy and translucent and just pushing through enough until I was on 'the other side'.

While holding his hand in this physical reality I could move about at will as the other Being in the other reality. I discovered that my name in that world is Alathara and that I was quite young in their years, that I had indeed been a messenger for most of that life and that I wasn't regarded as coming from any particular family or clan, but rather belonged with everyone.

I'm not sure that its possible to convey to you just how beautiful this other reality is or how thrilling it was to experience it that initial time and then be able to revisit it at will. In this case, words really do fail to describe the feeling of it all.

I also hope that you can appreciate how personal and private this story is to me, and how strange it feels for me to share it. Sharing my name from that reality is a particularly difficult thing for me to do, but I must share it because connecting with my parallel life has made an important difference for me and maybe it will make a difference for you too.

My relationship with this wonderful man did not last in this reality, but both of us believed we had been brought together for a reason and I felt very blessed by the whole experience and by his openness in exploring our concurrent lives further.

For me the benefits of knowing myself as 'also Alathara' have been powerful if subtle. Each time I connect with my lifetime in that reality, I feel that I am being infused with a positive energy and knowledge rather than learning something in an intellectual sense.

My life has taken some interesting turns since then and I received confirmation of my concurrent life most unexpectedly about a year later.

After several years of holding my five-day residential retreat at the same venue in Australia, I was told by the owner that they had to close for renovations and that I couldn't bring my group there that coming October. I went into panic mode as the course was almost fully booked and some of the students had already made their travel arrangements. I had to not only find a venue that could host us to our requirements, but it had to be a similar price, available on those exact dates and in the same location. Impossible!

Two days after delivering his bombshell, the owner emailed me and said 'Have you tried Chiltern Lodge?' I hadn't because I'd never even noticed it during all of those years. I had been driving past the road leading to Chiltern Lodge on my way to the venue I'd always used without even knowing it.

Naturally I called Chiltern Lodge right away and they could supply everything I needed, so with great relief I booked the group in for October. On the second day of the course I finally made some time to stroll around the grounds. The Lodge is set on over three acres of largely untouched Australian bush land, so the trees and wildlife are beautiful. As I meandered along one of the tracks a large tree caught my eye and I hurried in her direction and there she was, the same tree from my concurrent life!

I was breathless with excitement and felt so happy. No symbols appeared on her bark but I felt her welcome me and I knew I was in the right place. It was truly an amazing feeling.

That initial introduction to my other life and other self is an experience I will never forget and is now a place that I can deliberately choose to return to for inspiration and guidance

So that has been my own personal experience with my concurrent life, but what about you? How can you be sure you have a parallel life and what good might it do you to know?

It is as yet unclear to me if everyone has a concurrent life and if this is something constant, common or occasional. In the past five years I have had only a handful of clients whose concurrent lives were revealed during a reading, on average around 10 people per year. But its not statistics we're after, its experiences to help us move beyond our often limited thinking, understand ourselves better, evolve spiritually and attain higher states of awareness.

My recommendation is to keep an open mind and be willing to explore. Try this simple exercise with a clear intention and allow your Higher Self to take over, it will know if it's the right time for you to discover your own concurrent life.

EXERCISE THIRTEEN

TUNING IN TO YOUR PARALLEL LIFE

REQUIREMENTS: a quiet place where you can sit or lie comfortably
Pen and Notebook or Journal

TIME REQUIRED: 10–20 minutes

- Sit or lie down comfortably in a relaxed, private place.

- Focus on your desire and intention to learn something about your concurrent life, then ask you Higher Self and your Angels and Spirit Guides to assist you and guide you.

- Be open to the possibility that your experience will be very subtle. If you expect a feature length movie with lots of fanfare you might miss the subtler aspects of what you are being shown or what you're feeling.

- Remain relaxed, breathe deeply and be patient. All the while holding your intention and asking for something about your concurrent life to be revealed to you.

- Stay with your focus and intention for about 15–20 minutes.

Note: if you prefer, you can go into this exercise in bed before you go to sleep and have the intention that your concurrent life will be revealed to you during sleep. After all this is a time when the monkey mind is far less active and the intuitive senses far more receptive.

- At the end of your 20-minute session, or when you wake up in your bed, write down everything you can remember from your experience. And I do mean everything because its important to be prepared for the fact that you may only perceive small impressions to begin with and then as you become more experienced and maintain your strong intention more will be revealed. Keeping notes enables you to refer back and to build on a body of information. It is so easy to forget these things once you enter the busyness of your normal day, so please don't let go of the little wisps of information that appear, they could be just the foundation that your intuition needs to build upon.

For my clients and myself the apparent benefits of tapping into and learning about a parallel life have been subtle to be sure. There have been no revelations about where to go or what to do next, no huge upheavals that have changed everything overnight. The benefits have instead been more like true miracles, the small and subtle miracles that happen to us and through us every day, that we barely even notice.

These are the miracles that cause the wheels of our lives to keep turning, that line us up with the people we are destined to meet, put us in exactly the right place at the right time and continually shower us in all the blessings we often take for granted.

A concurrent life, and having some knowledge of it, is a momentous and potentially life changing thing, but I suggest that you approach it with awe and amazement rather than something you hope might solve the problems in your life.

These days I travel the world with my work, doing readings and giving courses and workshops in several different languages. I often find myself being drawn to beautiful trees, groves and forests such as the jungles around Iguazú Falls in Argentina, the beautiful Pineta on the coast of Tuscany, the majestic redwoods of northern California and the National Parks surrounding my home here in Australia.

Some years I am overseas, travelling constantly, for up to five months at a time, almost completely dependent on the hospitality and generosity of the friends, clients and students who invite me to share their homes. This all sounds a little bit like my life as Alathara, wouldn't you say?

Who knows just how much knowledge, guidance and high vibration I received from those symbols on that magical tree? And who knows just how much influence my concurrent life is having on me here in my Earthly life as BelindaGrace.

CHAPTER 11

Healing self-sabotage – your personality aspects

'I was having a very difficult time at work because of one woman there who had taken a strong dislike to me. With Belinda's help I discovered that this woman was a reflection of the deeply negative attitudes I had about myself. Once I learned how to heal my Self-critical aspect my work situation changed dramatically and this lady simply let me be. I had been on the verge of resigning and now I am happy in my work again. Healing this negative aspect was a big help to me.'

JACINTA

When you think about it you are not just one type of person. You will have many different facets or aspects to your personality that come into play in various situations. For instance very few people are extroverted or organised all the time, they will have days when they feel more introverted and require some solitude, or have one area of their life which is confused or even chaotic.

Most human beings are actually quite paradoxical creatures, full of inconsistencies and contradictions. To me this is a much more preferable way to be as I have never wanted to be squashed into one pigeonhole, yet for some reason there seems to be a belief floating around our culture that you have to be able to define yourself and who you are in one sentence. Human beings are not one dimensional, we are wonderfully complex and rich.

Included in this melange of 'who we are' are the parts of ourselves that we like and want everyone else to see, such as the efficient, the positive and the successful. However we also have, tucked away in the deep drawers and unused cupboards of our complex inner world, the parts of ourselves that we have labelled weak, unlovable, unworthy . . . and the list goes on.

No matter how cleverly you have buried or disguised them they will be having an effect on your life, often without you consciously realising it. In fact I have observed that the aspects most strenuously ignored or denied are the ones that have the most power. It was a wise person who once observed 'What you resist persists'.

In this chapter you are going to discover how to stop resisting the parts of yourself that you consider unacceptable. Once you do that you will find that these inner sabotage monsters will transform and start working for and with you rather than against you.

Not long ago a woman in her 40s came to see me for the first time. She had been divorced for about a year, had three children all under 10 years old living with her, and her ex-husband was, to say the least, not pulling his weight. I did not know any of this at the time. She had smiled at me sweetly when she came into my room and was very polite as she detailed for me some of her worries and woes.

It was not so much what she was saying that interested me though, because I was becoming increasingly fascinated by the show that was going on in her eyes. There was so much anger in them and with my clairvoyant sight I could literally see flames and sharp knives jumping out of her pupils! They weren't directed at me personally of course, it's just that there was so much anger in her system that her Anger Aspect had created this outlet for its self expression.

My Angels kept saying to me `Ask her what she is so angry about', so I did and it was like the whole room shook; she actually braced herself by grabbing the couch with both hands. Then she said to me `You weren't supposed to see that, I thought I had that all very well hidden'. She was amazed that it was so obvious to me, as we had been together for less than five minutes.

My consultations only last for one hour, so there was no time to waste. We introduced her to her Anger Aspect and it was a pretty wild ride. This aspect which she believed was so neatly tucked away began tearing the place apart. On my Inner Screen I could see it smashing the furniture into twigs, screaming, yelling and pounding its fists upon the floor. The tirade of angry words that it spoke through me was also very revealing, because much of its anger was directed not just at her ex-husband, but at men in general; particularly her father who had walked out on the family when she was 12, never to be seen again.

My client's Angry Aspect spat abuse at all men, who it regarded as irresponsible and worthless. This aspect was also angry at my client for getting married and setting herself up for what it believed was her inevitable disappointment and suffering. It is fortunate that our personality aspects remain non-physical, because they can certainly be very intense and powerful when they emerge. Although that is not to say they don't show up in our physical lives. In this woman's case, for instance, she had a knack for attracting angry behaviour from other people, whether it was from a complete stranger in another car or the people that she worked with.

In the last year she had fallen out with friends, been the victim of numerous episodes of road rage and had to be moved to another department in her company because of the bad vibes between her and some of her colleagues. She would have had suppressed anger prior to her divorce, but since the divorce it had multiplied tenfold and was acting like an irresistible magnet for people who wanted to vent their own anger.

The relief from her Anger Aspect came fairly swiftly after the session because she did her homework and observed this aspect regularly until it transformed. She was ashamed of her angry feelings and had hoped she could hide them, as we all do with the things that we don't like about ourselves. It takes courage to begin to understand the energies at play in your personality, but when you do it can be incredibly liberating.

That day in my office she was greatly relieved to finally have these feelings out in the open as we watched and listened to the fury that poured out of her angry self. Her Angels explained to her that there was no need to feel ashamed or believe she was a bad, angry person.

They told her that these personality aspects are created when we are very young and unable to deal with a painful or frightening situation.

In my client's case her father's departure had been the last straw in an unhappy relationship with him. The anger she had felt as a little girl about the way he treated her mother, her siblings and herself was painful and impossible to rationalise. She knew that her father wouldn't listen to her, so apart from the occasional outburst, she began to bottle all of those feelings up.

As I have heard the Angels explain many times, the Angry Aspect was formed by her subconscious mind as a survival mechanism. Each aspect acts as a storage space for the various emotions, until the individual is mature and strong enough to deal with them at a conscious level.

Very interesting things can start to happen when you own and heal your negative aspects. In this case a man in my client's office asked her out on a date a few months after her first treatment, and his comments were very telling.

When she asked him why he had waited to ask her out, he told her that she had always seemed a bit prickly and unapproachable, but that there was something a little softer and more open about her now. He had picked up on her anger towards men, even though he would not have labelled it that way, and had been afraid that she would snap at him.

She began to understand how all the anger that she had suppressed since her childhood had helped to set her up for a series of relationships with uncaring men, and then ultimately, no relationship at all.

Often people will say to me that they can now see that a particular aspect has been trying to get their attention for years by creating certain situations over and over again. We attract to ourselves what we carry inside; no amount of frozen smiles or political correctness can fool the Universe.

Percentage wise my client's angry self was perhaps only 1 per cent of who she was, but the so-called negative aspects are very powerful and can end up running your life if you don't pay attention to their messages.

So how can you get some clues as to what aspects in you need healing? Start by looking at what you attract into your life on a daily basis; the things that you don't like are not the Universe's way of punishing you, it is a red flag being waved from inside of you, from a part of you that needs your help.

Each personality aspect is like a coin, because it has two sides. The positive or flip side of the Angry Aspect is passion, including sexual passion, feistiness and an ability to stand up for yourself in appropriate ways. All pretty useful qualities wouldn't you agree? However you can't bury one side of the coin without burying the other, so when you suppress your anger you also suppress your capacity for living your life with passion, when you suppress hatred you suppress your capacity to feel love, when you suppress resentment you suppress your wellspring of forgiveness, and so on, and emotional deadness is the result.

When given the right kind of attention your negative aspects will automatically transform into the positive version of themselves. It is all a matter of degrees, as very few people feel all hatred and no love, but whatever hatred there is can be transformed back into love so that their capacity to give, receive and feel love becomes greater. That makes this one of the most uplifting techniques that I have been given the privilege to work with, because it clearly illustrates that even the darkest parts of us want to make their way back to the Light.

Here is a brief list of some of the negative personality aspects we have come across and their positive transformations:

NEGATIVE	**POSITIVE**
Anger	Passion, feistiness, ability to stand up for oneself
Hatred, including self-hatred	Love and self-love
Resentment	Forgiveness
Self-loathing	Self-acceptance

HEALING SELF-SABOTAGE – YOUR PERSONALITY ASPECTS

NEGATIVE	**POSITIVE**
Self-sabotage	Personal empowerment, success, ability to receive the good things in life
Poverty, lack and struggle	Abundance and trusting the flow of life
Pessimism	Optimism
Self-criticism	Confidence
Grief	Joy and happiness
Persecution, feeling picked on or hard done by	Harmony, sense of belonging
Greed	Gratitude and generosity
Fear	Trust and inner strength, feeling safe in the world
Sadness and depression	Happiness and inner peace
Abandonment, outsider, misfit	Knowing you belong, greater ability to connect with others
Victim, blaming	Responsible for your decisions and choices
Unappreciated	Appreciation of yourself
Superiority	Understanding, approachability, empathy
Jealous, envious, possessive	Trusting, grateful, abundant, generous, feeling safe
Judgemental	Non-judgemental, accepting, live and let live attitude
Wounded child	Sensitive child
Shame, loathing of life and self	Self-love, self acceptance, inner peace

So can you now begin to grasp what amazingly multi-faceted beings we are? The list seems endless and the combinations and degrees of expression of each aspect are unique to each person. Naturally we are all endowed with many positive aspects as well, such as generosity, kindness, empathy, compassion, curiosity, playfulness, wisdom, creativity, inventiveness, genius and so on. It is all there in each one of us, it just depends on which 'side of the coin' is more active; as the extent to which someone is stingy is also the extent to which they could become generous, or the extent to which they fear emotional commitment is also the extent to which they long for it.

Working with your own personality aspects will help you to unravel your own frustrating complexities and help you to express the highest versions of who you are in this life.

There is no limit to the number of aspects you can work with, the list in this book is just a sample of what I have come across. You will also discover your own, so be prepared to go with the flow as that wonderful imagination of yours helps you to connect with what is going on inside you.

The number of observation sessions required to transform an aspect is unique to each person, so try not to put limits on your inner work. Sometimes you will be pleasantly surprised at how quickly one evaporates, while others will be much more tenacious. Count your blessing that they are showing up and that more and more of your own personal energy is transforming into Light. Others will notice the difference in you, and you will certainly notice the positive changes in your self and the quality of your life.

The transformation process

As is the case with all the techniques that my Angels and Spirit Guides have taught me over the years, this one is actually quite simple. It will be new and unusual to you at first, but that doesn't mean it is difficult to do. My Angels and I have taught hundreds of people how to do this over the years and they have all benefited from it.

In this process it is very important to let your imagination flow and give it free rein, as it will be translating your suppressed emotions into images and words for you to experience. The whole basis of this process is observation, meaning that when you relax, close your eyes and focus on your Inner Screen, you will be able to observe one of your aspects as though you were watching it on television.

It is important to understand that the simple act of observing this part of yourself will allow it to heal. It has been denied and hidden away for almost all your life, expressed only through stress and the occasional outburst. The act of observance means it is no longer hidden or ignored but acknowledged with compassion. This compassion is what allows it to be released and transformed into it's positive manifestation.

The Angels always advise us that we must observe these wounded aspects of ourselves with detached compassion, acknowledging their presence without judgement, while this aspect of yourself finally gets the chance to reveal itself and come to you for help. You don't have to do anything other than observe, meaning that you listen to, watch and feel this part of you as it expresses itself without hindrance.

Observing means to have a sense of, to be aware of, to let it play out inside you without trying to interfere or change it. The true meaning of observation in this case is full attention with detached compassion.

Let's also define the meaning of the word detached in this situation, because some people mistakenly feel that it is something like being aloof. Detachment isn't the same as not caring, it is about respecting the way that this part of you needs to express itself, giving it permission to rant, rave, swear, cry, accuse or whatever it needs to do without trying to fix or change it. Put detached and compassion together and what you have is acceptance and understanding. That is all that these parts of you need – your acceptance, understanding and of course your attention – in order to heal.

EXERCISE FOURTEEN

OBSERVING NEGATIVE PERSONALITY ASPECTS

REQUIREMENTS: a quiet space where you can lie or sit comfortably

TIME REQUIRED: 15–30 minutes

- Sit or lie down somewhere that you can feel comfortable and relaxed.

- Focus on an area or an issue in your life which regularly causes you problems. It may be that you are always broke, that your relationships never last very long, or that you are always having conflicts with a certain person or type of person. Think more about the actual situation rather than trying to figure out which personality aspect you should be looking at. Everyone is different, there is no formula I can give you, only your Higher Self or subconscious wisdom will know which aspect you need to see most at this time, it may even be more than one, so be open to whatever comes.

Note: you cannot force an aspect to reveal itself. By focusing on the actual problem you create an opening for whatever aspect(s) wants to show up.

- ◆ Set your intention to observe one of these aspects of yourself with detached compassion. Be clear with the intention to not judge, analyse or try to change it in any way. The Universe takes care of the healing, all you have to do is give it your attention.

- ◆ The next step is to make your connection to your Guidance through your Channel, so allow yourself a minute or two to feel the light and energy coming down from the Cosmos and up from the Earth.

- ◆ Focus on your Inner Screen and ask your Angels and Spirit Guides to help you see the aspect that is ready to reveal itself, and just remain relaxed and attentive.

Note: On your first attempt it may take a few minutes before you get a sense of anything. Don't be impatient, these parts of your personality are accustomed to feeling unwanted and hiding themselves away. Give them a chance to adjust to the idea that you are now ready to acknowledge them.

- Gradually you will get a sense of some figure or character emerging, if your clairvoyant sight isn't very clear yet it can be like a feeling that someone has arrived. You know, a bit like when you know that someone has come into the room without even having to look around; you simply feel their presence.

- Stay as relaxed and focused as you can, continuing to breathe deeply and remain aware of your intention. You will receive some impressions; let your aspect express itself in any way it likes. It cannot actually touch or harm you no matter how strong its energy is.

- Enjoy your observation time, look for all the detail you can, tune in to how you are feeling within yourself – do you suddenly feel angry or sad? Listen attentively as though someone is about to say something very important, and just let the information come.

    The sad, depressed and victimised ones may be nothing much more than a sobbing heap on the floor. Your imagination will find some amazing ways to translate the energy of your suppressed emotions to you, like characters from the high dramas of your life. The Anxious Aspect might be in a small room pacing the floor, a Fear Aspect might be hiding behind a door, a Lonely Aspect may look like an aging cowboy trudging through the desert on his own, or a Judgemental Aspect may be sitting behind a huge desk banging a gavel.

- How long the observation process goes on for is up to you or your aspect. The aspect may suddenly fade away to indicate that today's viewing is over; another way to know when to stop is when the aspect starts to repeat the same information over and over. The only thing that each aspect knows is the emotion that it is created from. They are one dimensional and cannot relate to or express anything else, so eventually it will be like watching the same footage that keeps repeating in a loop because the aspect will have nothing else to say.

Ultimately, your own ability to stay attentive and focused is most important. If you are tired or concerned about running out of time then you can stop whenever you like. You simply ask your Angels and/or Spirit Guides to come and take over for you, and they will come and surround that aspect in a cocoon of protective white light, taking care of your aspect until you are ready to observe it the next time.

Every observation session will transform that aspect to some degree. Again there is no formula, but generally speaking one of two things will happen. Each time you go in and observe you will notice a slight alteration to your aspect.

Let's use a Depressed Aspect as an example. It may start off very morose and negative, looking heavy and dark, but each time you go in and observe it there is an increasing lightness about it and the negative monologue is not so intense. Eventually, from session to session you actually witness the stages of the transformation process, until all you are shown when you ask to observe your Depressed Aspect is the happy and joyous aspect of yourself.

The other method that has been taught to us is that the negative aspect will simply fade away more with each observation until eventually there is nothing to observe when you call up the Depressed Aspect. It is like the movie has ended and there is nothing more to show.

Either way, you will know that that aspect of yours is healed because you will see the transformed version, or your screen will simply be blank. And of course, something else will be different too, you will feel much better within yourself, and attract more positive people and situations into your life, because the energy you are giving out is a lot brighter.

It is important to note that healing a Depressed Aspect for instance, does not mean that you can't get depressed again. What you have healed is the baggage you have been carrying around for so long, clearing out the old store to give yourself a fresh start. You will always be capable of feeling any of the negative emotions associated with the negative aspects, having access to the full range of emotions is part of being human.

People often say to me 'I want to get rid of my grief' or 'I want to get rid of my anger' as though it is like a bad tooth that I could just pull out. The emotions are not like that, the 'bad' ones can't just be removed. They are there as a very important part of your intuitive guidance system that helps you to know when you are doing something that is right for you or not. If you want to be on your so-called highest or most spiritual path in this life then learn to listen to your feelings and emotions. One of the ways we learn about our positive emotions is by experiencing their opposites as well.

Feelings of anger can be a signal that you are in a situation that is unhealthy in some way, feelings of sadness can indicate that you are suppressing your lifelong dreams and not following your heart, just as sure as the intense sensation of heat can indicate that you are about to get burnt! So don't wish your negative emotions away, they are not bad in and of themselves, they only become negative when they are so suppressed that they covertly begin to run your life.

A negative personality aspect revealed

'I JUST CAN'T FIND ANYONE I LIKE . . .'

This was the lament of a man in his late 20s who had been seeing me for some time. He was shy, soft spoken and even quite withdrawn, and after having gotten to know him a little it didn't surprise me that he didn't socialise much.

I just assumed it was because he needed to work on his confidence. So we began the session and very quickly an aspect of his emerged that took me by surprise. It was his Arrogant Aspect and it was certainly in full flight.

For the next 20 minutes it spoke through me about all the things it didn't like about the people my client knew. According to this aspect they were all inferior to him in some way and not worth the effort or time it took to develop or maintain their friendship.

This Arrogant Aspect also spoke of how it refused to demean itself by doing work that it didn't want to do, or even to submit to the kind of questioning most of us consider normal in an interview. Its attitude was 'I am better than you and I don't have to prove it, if you can't see how superior I am then that's your problem.'

The image I was given of this aspect was of a tall, haughty, middle-aged male, like someone you would expect to see in the British Civil Service or a member of the aristocracy. He even spoke with a formal tone that was nothing like my client's normal voice. My client and I even started to giggle at some of the things that were said because they were so snobbish and absurd.

To his credit, my client completely owned the fact that he had always felt that way about other people on some level. Yes, he was genuinely shy and had some issues with feelings of inferiority as well, but he confessed that he knew his arrogance had been there all along and he had often thought of himself as arrogant.

He also admitted that this was indeed one of the reasons that he had not had a job in over a year, preferring to live on the money he made from playing the stock market.

He went home and continued the transformation of his Arrogant Aspect with his own observation sessions, and after a few weeks this aspect did not show up any more, but a new aspect did. The aspect of fear.

Healing his Arrogant Aspect had paved the way for his Fear Aspect to reveal itself, specifically his fear of people. When the new aspect showed itself my client asked his Angels what kind of aspect it was. They told him it was fear, which correlated with the feelings he had when the new aspect first appeared. He went to work observing this aspect, which gradually resulted in some very deep healing.

He is 30 now and is finally feeling strong enough to work, and to live in a place of his own, knowing that he has the tools for self-awareness and healing within him at all times.

FURTHER READING ON THIS SUBJECT:

Embracing Ourselves: The Voice Dialogue Manual by Hal and Sidra Stone
Sacred Contracts by Caroline Myss

CHAPTER 12

Creating heart and mind balance

> *'In the weeks after my partner left me for someone else I was so distraught that I could barely function. My heart was broken and I could not think clearly. I received a Heart Mind Balance during my first session with Belinda and continued to do them for myself whenever I could. It helped me to feel so much stronger and clearer; able to pull myself together and move on. I felt balanced instead of torn by the previous conflict between my heart and head.'*
>
> **TRACEY**

Without even realising it, most of us these days live mainly in our heads. We are often unaware of the stresses we put our bodies under through lack of exercise or excessive intake of stimulants such as coffee or alcohol. Often we are even more unaware of our true feelings about many of the most important matters in our lives. Or, if we are aware of our feelings it may still be difficult to express them clearly to others.

In the chapter on Psychic Conversations you learned how to use a tool which can help you to communicate messages that might well be sensitive or volatile in nature. In this chapter you will learn a technique that will help you to express your truth from another level of your being; the level of your heart.

Feeling blocked or embarrassed when it comes to expressing your gentleness and love can create just as many problems in this life as not being able to express your hurt or anger. The Heart-Mind balance will help you to express your heartfelt feelings more comfortably and calm your mind, so that the kind of fear that we justify by labelling it logical or rational will no longer dominate your life.

CREATING HEART AND MIND BALANCE

Once again, the Heart-Mind balance is a technique that was taught to me by my Angels and Spirit Guides while I was working on a client. Since that time it has been useful in many people's treatments and has become one of the techniques that I teach in all of the courses that I run.

It is such a simple process, easy to do for yourself or for another, and its benefits are numerous. If you are very worried about something, have problems with feelings of anxiety, have trouble making decisions or lack confidence in those decisions, then you can benefit from this technique.

Your heart always knows what to do even when your mind is confused. The Heart-Mind balance strengthens the heart while calming the mind, helping you to feel clearer and more connected to your truth.

Obviously we are not talking about the physical heart that pumps blood all around your body. We are talking about that profound part of you that is represented by the heart chakra, the part of you that feels and expresses love. Look around you now to witness the effects that too much living from the mind has had on our world: conflict, complicated bureaucracies and an overemphasis on material wealth and being 'in control'.

Take a moment now to imagine a world where more people lived consistently from their hearts, expressing their love and appreciation, being more receptive emotionally and more aware of the feelings of others. If global change seems a little ambitious to you, think again, because all great change begins with the individual. When your heart energy is strong, clear and flowing through your life, you will influence many other people in positive ways and you will create a more harmonious life for yourself.

When performing a Heart-Mind Balance you should sense a continuous flow of energy between the heart, throat and brow chakras. This energy flow forms the infinity symbol or figure 8, with the throat chakra in the middle being the point where the 8 crosses over itself.

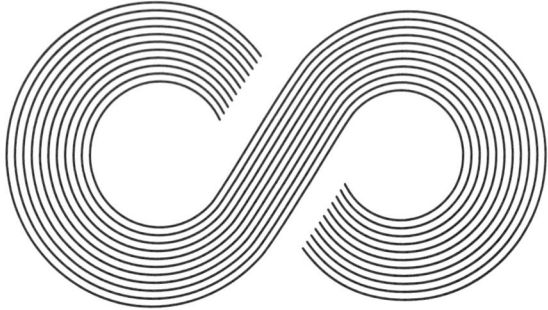

There is a very good reason why the flow of energy crosses over at the throat forming the figure 8 pattern, as the throat chakra is at the crossroads of the heart and the mind, dealing with a double dose of energy and often being the central point in a continuous tug of war.

As you clean up the energy which flows around the Heart-Mind configuration the throat chakra receives a much needed double dose of healing, as it is often very stressed or tense from years of domination by the mind energies and suppression of emotions and feelings. Human beings place a great deal of importance upon verbal communication, so our throat chakras are usually required to work very hard in order to help us get the things we say 'right' rather than expressing our truth or our true feelings. The following exercise will help you express your truth more clearly, straight from your heart.

As with any of the techniques in this book you may do whatever you like to set the scene and help yourself feel more confident and comfortable. If you have some favourite crystals that you would like to place nearby, then please do so. Light a candle put on soft music or burn some oils or incense. Ask your Angels and Spirit Guides to gather closely around you before you begin if that helps you feel more confident. It's your space, so make it all as pleasant as you like, and/or ask the person that you are working on what they feel may be beneficial for them.

EXERCISE FIFTEEN

CREATING YOUR OWN HEART-MIND BALANCE

REQUIREMENTS: a quiet location where you can lie or sit comfortably

TIME REQUIRED: 15–30 minutes

- Sit or lie quietly, close your eyes and breathe deeply, relaxing yourself and preparing for your visualisation. Set a clear intention to give yourself a lovely Heart-Mind balance.

- Take a moment to remember your connection to your Divine Guidance via your Channel and spend a minute or two getting yourself connected to the white light coming down through you from the Cosmos, and the warm, reddish light coming up to you from the core of the Earth.

- Imagine your Angels or Spirit Guides gathering around to support you.

- Now that you have engaged your antenna, take your attention to your Inner Screen as well, remembering that you have this place in your mind where images can be shown to you.

- Focus on your brow, throat and heart chakras. Imagine a figure 8 connecting the three of them with the throat chakra in the centre at the point where the figure 8 crosses over.

- Trace this figure 8 over your own chakras with your fingertips if you like, to get a feel for where it sits, coming up from your heart, crossing over at the throat, looping up and around through the brow and then back down through the throat again in the other direction, returning to the heart and so on, in a continuous flow.

Note: This is the energy pattern that you will be working with to create more balance between your heart and mind. Just like blood is constantly circulating through your arteries and veins, this energy is constantly flowing through this circuit that connects these three chakras.

- Relax, close your eyes and tune in to this energy flow. Imagine it on your Inner Screen if you like and see if you can get a sense of the colour and/or quality of the energy and the three chakras involved. Does the energy flow smoothly, or in fits and starts? How do the chakras feel, is one more blocked or heavy or tired than the others?

- Often the colour and quality of this energy is greyish, murky and sluggish. The brow chakra may feel overcharged and busy and the heart chakra may feel dull, weak, heavy or even numb. What you are aiming for is a smooth, steady energy flow that feels calm and strong, with no heaviness or blockages in any area, and a nice clean, bright colour to the energy rather than a dull or murky one.

- Once you are at the point where you have a little bit of a feeling for what is happening in your 'figure 8' and the three associated chakras, you can call in the healing energy and light to clear and balance it.

- Imagine a beautiful strong beam of violet light, or whatever colour feels best, flowing down to you from the Cosmos and into your heart chakra at the centre of your chest. Let it keep flowing from the heart chakra into the figure 8 until you feel that it has calmed, unblocked and brightened that energy flow. Imagine it soothing your mind, clearing your throat and strengthening your heart until the whole system feels refreshed and glowing!

- Finish off by surrounding yourself in a protective cocoon of silver or white light, taking a moment or two to enjoy the feeling of this healthy energy flow. Breathe deeply and become aware of your physical body again. Open your eyes.

Treating someone else

Once you have a feel for the Heart-Mind balance and have an understanding of how it works for you, it is quite a simple technique to perform on someone else. Ask their permission first, explain to them what it is about or have them read this chapter.

Even children as young as five or six will get the gist of what you are offering to do for them if you take the time to explain it in simple terms; you have read the instructions and it really is no more complicated than that. Focus upon your intention, which in this case is to give someone you care about a Heart-Mind balance.

Let go of your own opinions on their emotional state or their problems. Make it your intention to be the best and clearest Channel for the healing energy that you can be. Remember giving someone a treatment like this is not about you fixing them, but rather helping them gain the clarity and strength to help themselves.

EXERCISE SIXTEEN

TREATING SOMEONE ELSE TO A HEART-MIND BALANCE

REQUIREMENTS: a quiet location where your subject can sit or lie comfortably and can be easily accessed by you

TIME REQUIRED: 10–20 minutes

- Have the person lie down and close their eyes. Make sure that you can sit or stand comfortably alongside them.
- Ask your Angels and Spirit Guides to gather around and support you.
- Take a moment to feel your own connection to the Cosmos and the Earth through your Channel.
- Place your fingertips gently on any two of the three chakras involved in this technique – the heart, throat and brow – and imagine the cleansing violet light flowing down from the Cosmos, through your Channel and into your heart chakra.
- From there the light branches off to flow out through both your arms, passing through your shoulders, upper arms, elbows, forearms and wrists and then finally out through your fingertips and into the person you are working on.
- You are now a Channel or conduit for the energy and light, there is nothing else that you have to do except keep the flow going by continuing the figure 8 through the three chakras. As human beings our job is not to be the actual healer, but to strive to be

the clearest possible vehicle for the healing energies that the Universe naturally provides.

- Move your hands between the three chakras as you feel guided to do so, check in with your Inner Screen for any vision that might show up.

- Allow the healing energy to flow to you and through you, into their chakras. It is terrific if you can feel the spin of the chakras or the flow of the energy through your arms and hands or around their figure 8, but if you can't then once again I say to you don't worry. As long as your intention is clear then the Universe will take care of the rest.

- Look for the flow of energy through the figure 8 and see if you can notice it clear and change. Feel free to tell the person you are working on what is happening as you work, or wait until you have finished and then exchange feedback; whatever feels more comfortable for you.

- Ten or 15 minutes will be quite enough. When you are ready to finish imagine yourself wrapping them in a lovely soft cocoon of white energy and light, then take your hands away.

- Picture yourself standing under a waterfall of silver light that rinses away any energy that you may have absorbed into your field from them.

- Encourage them to lie or sit quietly for a minute or two before getting up.

- Make sure that you ask the person you treated to give you some feedback on what they experienced so that you can learn. You will also be thrilled to hear their reports of feeling warmed and soothed by the energy flowing from your hands.

A Heart-Mind balance restored

She couldn't say 'I love you.'

Not long after the Angels first taught me this technique a woman in her 30s came to see me in a considerable state of despair. She had been in a relationship with a man for around three years and had been very happy. Around 12 months before she came to see me her boyfriend had started to tell her that he loved her, and although he was disappointed that she didn't say those words back to him he figured that it was only a matter of time. He could feel that she loved him even though she never used those words.

Unfortunately her inability to say 'I love you' did start to become a problem. Her partner began to get angry and feel insecure, even accusing her sometimes of deliberately withholding or simply not loving him at all.

My client blurted all this out in a couple of minutes, crying all the while. She was afraid of admitting her feelings lest she be hurt again, like she had been in the past. My Angels very clearly told me that she needed a Heart-Mind balance, so I did what I was told and worked on her for half an hour or so.

As the treatment proceeded she became so calm and peaceful, her eyes closed, she didn't even realise that a gentle smile was beginning to form on her face. It wasn't necessary for me to say anything, so I just let the wonderful energy and light do its work.

Her heart energy was so constricted that I felt continually drawn to keeping one of my hands on her heart chakra. My other hand moved back and forth between her brow and throat. Slowly, the murky energy that moved sluggishly through her figure 8 became brighter and more vibrant, eventually achieving a lovely bluish/violet hue.

When it all felt clear and balanced we wrapped her in a cocoon of light and sent her on her way, with a happy expression where a very tense one had been less than an hour ago.

A week later she contacted me to tell me that her boyfriend had proposed! She had found the courage to say those magical three words, which was all he had really been waiting for. Feeling more connected to her now than he ever had before he decided to pop the question and they were both delighted, as I was for them.

Most of us are waiting around for big, earth shattering miracles to come along and totally transform our lives. When we think like this we usually miss the fact that smaller miracles are happening for us every day. As you learn to work with the techniques in this book, particularly the ones that most appeal to you, it will become apparent to you that the ability to affect some of these small miracles is in the palm of your hands. You have nothing to lose and much to gain, so practice, experiment, trust your inner guidance and enjoy.

CHAPTER 13

Do I have to meditate? – no, but it really does help!

> *'Dear Belinda*
> *I always knew I was intuitive, but didn't know how to start on my own wonderful journey. I communicate regularly with the guides you introduced me to, during my meditation time and as I am going about my business day to day. I feel happier and more confident now because I can ask for, and receive help any place, any time.'*
>
> **GLENDA**

You probably weren't expecting a chapter on meditation in a book about developing your psychic abilities, but the benefits of meditation are very wide ranging, especially when you wish to become more intuitive and clairvoyant.

Most of us lead very busy lives and become all too 'accustomed' to almost unrelenting noise and activity. Constant mental activity often takes the form of planning for the future or worrying about the past, which can create a low-level anxiety that you live with each day and come to believe is normal. Yet it is in the quiet times that your Divine Guidance will reach you most easily. Remember the ringing in my ears at three or four o'clock in the morning?

Many people find their early attempts at meditating dull and frustrating. We are so familiar with thinking all the time or having something going on around us to entertain or distract, that inner silence is very unfamiliar territory. I know meditating can be difficult at first, but eventually you will come to wonder how you ever got along without it.

Meditation is a way of quieting the clamour of the mind while resting your body and mind together at one time. As a result of regular meditation many people experience a greater sense of inner calm, improved concentration, more refreshing sleep and even physical benefits such as the lowering of blood pressure or the improvement of certain illnesses or conditions.

Taking the time out to meditate may seem to be a problem for very busy people at first. It may even seem to be a waste of time because nothing appears to be 'happening'. For most of us, any kind of endeavour can only be considered fruitful when it produces something obvious and tangible. But the 'nothing happening' part of meditation is really the key, as it gives your mind time to rest and unravel for a while.

Some of the most successful, effective, efficient and productive people that I know meditate regularly. Corporations all around the world are now paying for their top employees to learn how to meditate so that they are calmer and able to focus their minds better on their work.

These companies and their CEO's and MD's might not think of these practices as meditation; perhaps they have a catchier and more modern label such as 'mind focusing technique', but it is all meditation no matter how you package it.

If you are an ambitious, goal-oriented person or if you simply want to get more out of your life and create a sanctuary of peace within yourself that is available to you 24 hours a day, then I recommend that you begin to meditate in some way. Once a day is great, but you will benefit from it even if you only manage occasional practice.

How do I meditate?

There is no one 'right' way to meditate, but all forms of meditation do involve focusing the mind in some way. One of the greatest obstacles to meditation for many people seems to be the idea that you must sit cross-legged, completely immobile and in silence and isolation. This approach, quite understandably, is somewhat daunting and unappealing. It simply isn't possible for all of us to behave like yogis, what is important is that meditation becomes an enjoyable practice for you.

There is nothing wrong with meditating when you are seated, curled up on the couch or stretching out in bed. You can meditate on the bus on your way to work, or while you are working on your tan at the beach. If you close your eyes and breathe deeply for five minutes during your lunch break, that can be a meditation.

Develop a realistic approach that allows your meditation practice to become an integral part of your lifestyle.

Interestingly, there are also many activities that can be undertaken as meditation. In many cultures meditation practices include walking, chanting, singing, eating, dancing and so on. If any of these activities gives you pleasure, then use them as part of your meditation practice.

Meditation is all about focusing your mind, especially when you are a beginner. As you are enjoying your walk along the beach or in the park, inhale and exhale deeply and focus your attention on the rhythm of your footsteps, the patterns in the sand or grass, the sound of the waves or birds, or anything else that absorbs your attention in a gentle and relaxing way.

Eating is the same. How often do you hurry through a meal, finish it and then don't even really remember enjoying it? Focus on your food; appreciate the beautiful colours, aromas and textures. Notice all the different flavours that come with every mouthful and don't take your attention from all this until the meal is finished.

By focusing your mind on a pleasurable activity, noticing the details and sensations in a simple or everyday act, letting the rhythm and energy of life flow through you as you flow with it, you are undertaking a form of meditation.

EXERCISE SEVENTEEN

A SIMPLE MEDITATION PRACTICE

REQUIREMENTS: a quiet place which is dark or softly lit where you can sit comfortably

Candle

Box of matches

TIME REQUIRED: 10 minutes

- Place your unlit candle in front of where you will sit.
- Seat yourself comfortably in front of the unlit candle. Breathe deeply and take a moment to relax.
- Light your candle, taking time to notice the sparking of the match or the dancing of the flame. Watch the flame as you move it to the candle wick and light it.
- Blow out the match and watch as the smoke drifts away.
- Focus your attention gently on the candle flame, do not stare at it, just let your gaze soften as you watch it.
- Allow your breathing to become deeper and slower.
- Give all your attention to the candle flame for several minutes. As other thoughts enter your mind just let them drift away rather than latching onto them.
- When you achieve a sense of quiet calm, your mind empty of all thoughts, sit quietly and contemplate the candle flame, noticing how it flickers or how the light diffuses around it.

- When you are ready to finish, take another deep breath, blink your eyes a few times and blow the candle out. Remain seated for a few moments, enjoying your state of relaxation before moving back into your general activities.

Other meditation techniques

One of the easiest ways to get into meditation is by listening to a recording of a guided meditation.

A guided meditation is just like a story that guides you through a relaxing series of images to help focus your mind in a soft and flowing way. Listening to a recording such as this gives your mind something to focus on without placing demands on you or forcing you to think.

There are many meditations available online, for example via YouTube or your music streaming platform. Some will have the voice of the facilitator only, some will have music only and most will have both, so make sure you read the description on the cover first and choose one that focuses on topics or themes that you will find helpful.

On my own meditations, for example, there are five different meditations ranging in length from around nine minutes to 16 minutes. Each meditation has a different theme, such as helping you to become more aware of the Angels that surround you, or guiding you on a peaceful journey through a beautiful, enchanted forest.

You may also like to try meditating in silence or with your favourite, soothing music playing softly, allowing the beauty of the sounds to transport you to a more harmonious inner state.

Instead of trying to empty your mind and 'think about nothing', an easier method is to simply focus your mind on a peaceful theme or image. Use your imagination to help you feel like you are floating in the clouds or sitting on a mountainside surrounded by flowers and endless natural beauty. Whatever appeals to you at that moment is fine.

If other thoughts intrude, gently let them go and return to your pleasant meditations.

Another useful technique is to repeat a word or short phrase over and over in your mind, rolling it over in your thoughts like a pebble in a stream. It may be a word with a lot of meaning, such as 'love', 'joy' or 'peace' or a phrase with great healing power such as 'I forgive myself' or 'I love myself'. This will help to keep your mind from wandering off in other directions.

When meditating in complete silence just let whatever thoughts or memories that want to surface come up and float away. Rather than getting drawn into one train of thought, allow your thoughts to float through your mind and imagine them evaporating or being blown away like small clouds on a summer breeze.

Meditating in silence can be truly amazing because it gives you a glimpse of all the memories and feelings that you have stored away within yourself throughout your life, and may give you some clues as to which Personality Aspects you may need to observe or insights into some of your past lives.

It can also be a wonderful time for ideas and inspiration. Keep your pen and notebook near you if you like, so that when you are finished you can jot down any helpful or creative ideas that might have come to you during the meditation. The power of silence creates the space for you to receive brilliant ideas, solutions to problems, prompts about something important and so on, because when the chatter of your mind slows down, your Angels, Spirit Guides and Divine Guidance is much more easily heard.

During meditation it is also beneficial to focus your attention on your breathing. Keeping your breath deep and rhythmic is one of the most effective ways to soothe yourself and remove your attention from the mind. Picture the air entering your body and flowing deep into your lungs, feeling its life-giving energy going into every cell.

If you have a sore, stiff or tense muscle or joint, or pain somewhere, then imagine your breath flowing to and through this area of your body and releasing that pain or discomfort.

The in-breath brings in healing light and energy and the out-breath takes the pain, tension or blockage away. At the very least, being more aware of your breathing will help to supply more oxygen to your body, warm you up, aid circulation and encourage you to breathe more fully throughout your life. Shallow breathing is just one of the unfortunate side effects of a stressful lifestyle, so breathe deeply while you meditate to reap the healing benefits.

Closing your eyes while meditating is probably preferable, as it encourages you to focus your attention inward and connects you with your inner world. It is also more relaxing, both for your eyes and your mind. If you prefer to keep your eyes open make sure your eyelids are soft and focus on something close to you like your hands or something attractive like a candle flame.

How often should I meditate?

Once a day is great if you can manage it, at a time that suits you. If you find it stressful to add another activity to your morning schedule then try meditating at night, as it can also help you have a more restful night's sleep.

Use your common sense and make it work for you. If you find that five or 10 minutes is your maximum to begin with that is fine. Eventually you will find that you can extend that time, or treat yourself to a nice long meditation while having a luxurious Sunday bath.

Combine meditation with things that you already enjoy doing, be inventive and don't put pressure on yourself to live up to someone else's standard. Plan your meditation times as times that are important for you and a wonderful way to benefit the development of your intuitive and psychic abilities. Enjoy!

FURTHER READING ON THIS SUBJECT:

Care of the Soul by Thomas Moore
Everyday Enlightenment: How to be a Spiritual Warrior at the Kitchen Sink by the Venerable Yeshe Chodron

CHAPTER 14

Our enlightened children

One day a client of mine, and her husband, came in for a Chakra Balance, and they brought their four-week-old daughter along. As I worked on the mother the baby slept, and I saw something that was completely new to my clairvoyant sight. The child had streams of rosy pink light flowing out from her heart chakra, reaching out and wrapping themselves around both parents, the child was sending them her love.

BELINDAGRACE

So now you have had the opportunity to discover some of your own natural intuitive and psychic skills, try to imagine what your life might have been like if you had known how to use them since you were a child.

Ponder this for a moment, because the differences and the possibilities are truly amazing. Do you think that your struggles would have been as difficult or lasted as long if you could have cleared some of your past lives in your teens?

Would you have felt so alone or frightened during the trying times if you had known how to connect and communicate with your Angels and Spirit Guides?

Is it possible that you might have had a stronger sense of self and your life purpose if you had known how to keep your chakras, Channel and Inner Screen open and strong?

Would you have been so easily swayed by other peoples' opinions if you had been able to receive Divine Guidance through automatic writing?

Is it possible that you would love and accept yourself more today if you had known how to heal and transform the negative Personality Aspects that caused inner and outer conflict in your life?

Children are naturally intuitive and clairvoyant, and in many ways the children of today are much more advanced in these areas than most adults. If you have children of your own or come into contact with them, you can be supportive of these innate skills even if you don't fully understand them.

When a child is born their physical body is 100 per cent here but they are still very strongly connected to the Light. Their crown chakra (fontanels) and Channel is very open and strong; it is as though they exist in two worlds.

As the days and weeks pass the soul gradually adjusts to the physical body that it has taken on in order to journey through yet another lifetime. At around the age of two to three years the adjustment process can become a little traumatic, as the intensifying focus on the physical life pulls them increasingly away from the previous realm they inhabited.

There is often a kind of rebellion against the relatively restrictive and heavy nature of physical life. The child is now expected to toilet train, eat more solids, feed itself and learn all the other basics of coping with the outside world, with increasingly less time available for the all important inner world and life.

The next, most noticeable stage of rebellion is usually the teenage years, and this is no coincidence. Since the age of two or three the child has continued to adjust to its new environment, but is generally still protected from many of life's demands by the parents. During the teen years however, it becomes very obvious to the child that it will soon have to fend for itself, and the increased demands of coping in the physical world takes the child even further away from his or her spiritual connections.

More and more the emphasis is on study, knowledge, logic, success, accumulation, achievement, competition, career, the future and so on.

The youngest person that I have worked with was seven years old. I have found whenever I have the privilege of working on one so young they easily comprehend the information that I Channel and my descriptions of what I am doing.

If I describe one of their Angels or tell them about the colours of their chakras, or clear a past life that has come up to be released, they often respond by saying that they already knew about it and had seen some of it before.

Parents often tell me about how their child sees clouds of colour around people (the aura), or how their young children 'just know things' without any logical way of having been informed. As adults we underestimate children all the time, and if we cannot understand their natural connection to the other dimensions that surround us we usually relegate it to the realms of imagination and fantasy. Something strange, even inconvenient, that they will eventually grow out of.

Teenage 'rebellion' is often dismissed as a lack of understanding about the way things are, and how the 'real' world works, but what are we defending? I believe that we should encourage their spiritedness and individuality instead of putting so much energy into forcing them to conform. Who knows, we might even be able to learn something from them!

Naturally, children need guidelines to help them with the process of growing up, and they can of course benefit from the experience of their parents and other elders. What they don't need is to be stifled by our fears or our ignorance. Encourage your children to talk about the things that they see and believe in that you might define as 'not real'. Ask them to describe it to you in detail and have the courage to acknowledge that anything is possible.

Help them to understand that they have chosen a journey here in the physical realm, so it is important to be on the best possible terms with life here on Earth, while reassuring them that they can maintain their connections to the unseen or non-physical realms as well.

Physical life is to be treasured, savoured and enjoyed, and is a journey that provides the opportunity for enormous spiritual growth, but it is not the only reality that we need to stay connected to during this lifetime. Eastern cultures have always known this. Concepts such as reincarnation and practices such as meditation are part of daily life, and many things that we Westerners still think of as weird or too 'out there' are ordinary to them.

Talk to your children about the fact that they have Angels and Spirit Guides around them, explore books on chakras with them, especially the ones with lovely, colourful pictures. Ask them what they understand about the idea of reincarnation and whether they feel they have lived here before.

More than once I have listened to a shocked client tell me about how their child knew what a certain location would look like, without the child having been there before in this life.

I once gave a small crystal to a child who had sores in her mouth because my Guidance told me that this particular stone would help heal those sores. 'Great!' I thought, 'She can hold onto the crystal or put it beside her bed, won't that be lovely'. To my surprise, this very aware two-year-old took the crystal from me, and with considerable gravity, explained that the stone would only help her if she held it in her mouth! When her mother and I both looked alarmed she reassured us that she would sit still while it was in her mouth and that she wouldn't swallow it.

Later that week, when her sores had cleared up and she was feeling better, her mother took her to a crystal shop where she confidently chose a selection for herself. The mother was amazed at the connection her child obviously felt with some of the crystals, and at how definite she was about wanting some and not others.

Another girl of around three years of age was delighted when I told her I love to hug trees. I picked her up and we hugged some beautiful ones together. She said she could feel their energy and that some of them spoke to her.

I guess what I am trying to say is that we can learn a lot from our children and the younger generations in general. Every person has their own special brand of wisdom, whether they are educated or not, 'spiritual' or not, young, old or somewhere in between. The young bring with them such incredible awareness and understanding in order to help the human race step up to a new level of consciousness.

Whether you call them Rainbow Children, Crystal Children or Indigo Children, it matters not, the wise ones are here, and the sooner we notice the better things will be for everyone.

There is a lovely saying that I am sure many of you already know, and it goes something like this: 'We are not human beings having a spiritual experience; we are spiritual beings having a human experience.' Our children know this, help them not to forget it, while you do your best to understand.

EXERCISE EIGHTEEN

LEARNING FROM OUR CHILDREN

REQUIREMENTS: a child (son, daughter, niece, nephew, grandchild or friend's child) who is happy to chat with you for awhile
A quiet place where you and the child can sit and talk

OPTIONAL: Paper, colouring pencils, crayons, markers

TIME REQUIRED: 10 minutes – or as long as you like

- Ask the child to tell you what they know about Angels, Faeries, Invisible or Imaginary Friends.
- Listen to what they say without contradicting or correcting them.
- Explain to the child that you would like to know more about your Guides or Angels and that you would like their help.
- Ask the child what they notice around you, without influencing what they may say. They may comment about colours, shadows or people around you, encourage them to expand on any of this without leading them.
- If they are willing, ask the child to draw what they are picking up on, using the materials provided.
- Once they have finished telling you or drawing, thank them for their help and let them know how special and clever they are.
- Treasure the information or pictures you have been given forever.

A child's belief revealed

Although we all know that children have a special connection with their pets, I was reminded how strong and loving a bond that can be when a friend of mine had to take a much loved family dog to the vet for a serious operation.

My friend and her husband were very upset and worried, fearing that their pet would not survive. They were equally worried about their daughter, who had a strong affection for the dog and would no doubt be devastated by his loss.

I went to speak to their daughter, who was only four years old, hoping to give her a hug and some words of comfort. I managed a few awkward comments before she smiled and put her hand on my arm, to reassure me.

'I'm not worried,' she said. 'I know he will be all right.'

I smiled at her calm face. 'How do you know that?' I asked.

'The Angels told me he would be fine,' she replied.

She was so bright-eyed, positive and certain that I knew I didn't have to say anything more to her.

A week later the dog came home from the vet, and just as the Angels had promised, he was in great shape. That was several years ago and the dog is still fine!

FURTHER READING ON THIS SUBJECT:

Indigo, Crystal and Rainbow Children by Doreen Virtue
The Sixth Sense of Children: Nurturing Your Child's Intuitive Abilities by Litany Burns
Emissary of Love: The Psychic Children Speak to the World by James F. Twyman
General recommended reading:
Conversations with God Books 1, 2 and 3, by Neale Donald Walsch
Communion with God by Neale Donald Walsch
Oneness: The Teachings by Rasha
Power vs. Force by David R. Hawkins
Autobiography of a Yogi by Paramahansa Yogananda

CHAPTER 15

Are you a star seed?

'Through meditation and connecting with my Angels and Guides, I began to remember who I was: a Universal Being incarnating in physical form on Earth and, in a split second my life changed. I felt as though I belonged and I knew that I was here for a reason.
Belinda began talking about Star Seeds. She said, "Actually Melissa, I think you are a Star Seed".
I was relieved to be able to talk about who I was.'

MELISSA

Over the last five or six years the number of star seeds who have found their way to me has been increasing. I find these people quite delightful and can often recognise them immediately by the distinctive, and sometimes other-worldly, shimmer in their eyes. Star seed eyes are often quite mesmerising to behold – intense, glassy, bright and with an air that says 'I live here on Earth but I'm not from here.'

As the number of star seeds coming to me for readings and attending my courses increased I would receive guidance for them about their situation and how to better understand themselves. Some of them have very strange experiences and interactions with this world and others simply feel that they don't quite fit in with the human race.

The most straightforward definition of a star seed that I can give you is this:

- ◆ A person whose last incarnation, before their current lifetime here on Earth, was in a completely different dimension and different civilisation. Put another way, their most recent past lifetime was not here on Earth as a human being, but in a civilisation and 'location' very different to our planet.

- They deliberately choose to incarnate on Earth to experience human life, and are coming back to have all the usual growth that human life affords non-star seed people, with the key factor being that they agreed to stay in touch with, or remain connected to their former civilisation throughout this, their current Earthly life. Why? So that their former civilisation can monitor and learn about life here on Earth and what it is like to be human.

- My Angels and Guides have described star seeds as akin to 'living wifi modems' who are constantly transmitting information back to their former civilisation. Without realising it, the star seed person has a strong connection to their former community and that community is learning about life here on Earth through them.

- The existence of this connection to their former civilisation can often create a feeling of 'belonging somewhere else' for the star seed. For example, numerous star seed clients have told me how they have looked longingly up at the planets and stars in our night skies, wishing they could 'go home'.

- Their former community usually wishes to study one particular area of human life through the star seed and again, it's important to realise that the star seed person agreed to all of this before they reincarnated on Earth. Thus we often see that the star seed person will have intense experiences or engagement with certain aspects of human existence; such as emotional highs and lows, learning difficulties or physical health issues.

- As the star seed's experiences are transmitted back to their former civilisation, that community learns more about how we live here, what it means to be human and of course the challenges faced on Earth. Why do they want to learn more about us? The response to this question from my star seed clients' Angels and Guides is that their former civilisation is 'holding a space' for the human race because they care about us and feel deeply for our challenges and struggles. They believe that if they better understand us, then they can better support us.

It is very easy for a star seed to be misunderstood in our culture. They can seem distracted, inattentive, almost always hyper-sensitive, they may withdraw from the world as a means of protecting themselves and their sensitivity, or they may just seem like they are always on a different wavelength. Thankfully more and more parents are realising that a child who demonstrates similar behaviours and attitudes isn't automatically difficult or unwell. Increasingly it's the parents of young children who come to me seeking support and answers.

If you are a parent and you think you might have a star seed on your hands, its important to remember that the vast majority of them manage very well and will actually do better if you encourage them to embrace a life that encompasses both of their worlds.

Do your own research, share their interest in the cosmos, talk with them open-mindedly about how they feel and how they perceive the human race and life on Earth. We have all lived on Earth before in other human lifetimes, yet what is less understood are the lifetimes we have in other dimensions, solar systems and even galaxies. If all of this seems like a lot to digest – don't worry. The most important thing to understand is that your star seed child will best respond to being listened to, and answering open questions, rather than being told how it is or should be for them. They will thrive under your support and love and your patience.

Being a star seed child or young adult is not, however, an excuse for poor behaviour. Your child did choose to return to Earth for another human incarnation and, even though they are also a star seed, it's important to remember, and to remind them, that they are a star seed human. This means that they have also come here in this lifetime to learn and grow just like everyone else and as children and young adults they still require all those essential things such as healthy boundaries, positive discipline, education, social skills, a sense of responsibility, physical health and fitness, friends and hobbies. Encouraging them to embrace the combination of being a star seed and a person will most likely be the best approach.

One of the most poignant things I have observed about star seed people thus far is that this world often feels like a very coarse and crass place to them. They find it harsh physically, emotionally, mentally, intellectually and of course spiritually. Life on Earth for a star seed person is like life with the volume continually turned up full blast. They may be afraid of people, they may find it difficult to connect and they will often feel inferior and superior to others at the same time – both stances being the flipside of the same coin. Which brings me back to the importance of involving star seed people in normal activities while at the same time encouraging them to embrace their star seed status.

> *'Before enlightenment chop wood, carry water.*
> *After enlightenment chop wood, carry water.'*
>
> **ZEN KOAN**

There is no doubt that star seed people are special, different, unusual and so on. But aren't we all? And don't we all face our own unique set of challenges in each lifetime? The above koan reminds us that even the most wise and aware among us must 'chop wood, carry water' in order to grow in this and every other lifetime. This physical reality demands 'chop wood, carry water' from all of us on many levels from simple personal hygiene to being responsible for the safety and welfare of others. Therefore one of the main goals for a star seed person must be the same as for all people – to create a life of healthy balance.

In this amazing digital age it is also possible for star seeds to seek one another out worldwide and lend each other support. While I haven't been able to survey the entire planet, my experience is that their numbers are growing.

Among the star seeds who I have met and worked with, I can genuinely say that they have all come here to their current lifetime from a civilisation that is vastly more advanced than our own. More often than not, these civilisations are non-physical and exist in a dimension or vibration rather than on a solid planet somewhere out in space. These dimensions sometimes appear crystalline in nature and they glow with the most exquisite light and vibrate to the most exquisite sounds. In these cases there is little sense of the kind of separateness we experience here on Earth and communication among their community happens via what we would recognise as thought.

They are fascinated by our experiences in this Earthly dimension and seem eager to learn more about how we love, function, think and feel. They are amazed by how we allow emotions to influence our behaviour and choices, by our relationships and attachments, by our materialism, our belief systems, our faiths and fears, our conflicts, our challenges and our capacity for greatness. They regard Earth as an incredibly precious place where Souls have the opportunity to experience an environment that is unlike any other in the universe.

In my experience none of these civilisations attempt to influence the star seed person's behaviour or choices. They simply want to learn all they can about us and receive the transmissions that the star seed facilitates as per their original agreement. Beyond that it is my impression that the community stays out of the star seed person's life so that they can experience their Earthly existence just as they choose.

Where this will all lead I cannot say, and there are myriad beliefs, fears and hopes out there about whether or not, one day, some sort of 'extra-terrestrial' civilisation will come to either save or destroy us. For me at least, this is not the point of a star seed existence, for me the point is two fold:

1) Through star seed people we stay in contact with other civilisations that have a positive interest in life here on Earth, and

2) Star seed people are here to experience human life, have their journey, process their karma and do their spiritual development work just like the rest of us.

Being a star seed person may seem to add another level of complexity to being human, but it does not confer any kind of elevated status – it's just another personal quality or trait. A star seed's longing for their cosmic home or feelings of not belonging are indeed heart-rending at times, yet no more so than the longing anyone might feel for a person or place they loved in a past lifetime or for our general, collective longing to return to our Source.

A star seed's very human journey

In 2015 I had the privilege of doing a reading for a young man who had just been released from prison. His story is an extraordinary one of personal suffering, family turmoil, loss, authoritarian reaction, crisis, support and recovery.

One year before I met him, when he was only 22 years old, his mother, who he adored, announced that she was terminally ill with cancer and would soon die. Incredibly she had known of her illness for almost two years, had been receiving some treatment while enduring a gradual decline and had somehow managed to keep all of this from her husband and son. To say that they were devastated is a gross understatement. Try to imagine the enormous tidal waves of anger, shock, grief and disbelief as you come to terms with the fact that not only is your mother terminally ill but that she has kept this from you since day one. My client and his father felt utterly powerless, totally betrayed, grief-stricken, guilt-ridden and unable to really process what they had just been told.

A mere two weeks later she died. And this second tsunami of emotional devastation caused the father and son to emotionally breakdown. They had all the paperwork to deal with, uncomprehending extended family and friends demanding answers and their own heartbreak as they tried to come to terms with their terrible and sudden loss.

Something had to give, and this young man, Andrew, ran amok. He drank heavily, vandalised property and eventually stole a car. He was arrested, put in prison and charged. One can only imagine how these events affected his father, a kind and open-minded man who had been a client of mine for about three years. The short version of this story is that Andrew was tried, convicted and given a suspended sentence of three years parole with community service work. Naturally his father was relieved that his son wasn't put back in prison for a longer term but the consequences were still deeply troubling. Andrew now had a criminal record and the community service hours required would cause him to struggle with the demands of his university degree. Things certainly didn't look rosy, and of course there was still all that painful unresolved emotion to deal with.

Andrew came to see me soon after his trial and conviction and I could tell from the first moment that it was going to be a powerful reading. His mother came through and spoke to him. His anger and grief were so intense it was like a solid mass in the room. He cried, he told me he hated himself and I could literally feel his heart breaking. Then, without warning the room all around me became filled with what I can only describe as semi-flexible strands of gel-like crystal and in my clairvoyant sight I saw Andrew being lovingly farewelled from a beautiful civilisation that existed within these crystalline formations. The formations were glossy and mostly plum, purple and ruby coloured, with occasional shimmers of midnight blue. It was so beautiful and peaceful in this other world.

Andrew's Angels and Guides came forth and told him he is a star seed and that the main thing his former community were observing through him was how males dealt with powerful emotions and experiences with justice and injustice. As I described the richly coloured crystalline world to Andrew, and conveyed the information, tears rolled down his face. When I was finally able to pause he told me that he had seen that crystalline dimension before. Immediately following his arrest he was put in the local prison for a few days. He was distraught, and left to himself for hours on end and he began to go in and out of consciousness. He began to see the exact coloured formations that I had described and had tried to picture them more clearly by closing his eyes while reaching out with his hands to try to touch them. Andrew instantly recognised the dimension I described.

Even though he found those formations comforting, and the energy that dimension emanated soothing, he was still frightened. He was alone in a prison cell, feeling terrible guilt over the trouble he was causing his already devastated father. So he told himself he must be hallucinating or going insane. He said nothing of this to anyone.

During his reading his Angels and Guides told him that he had agreed with his former civilisation to come to Earth as a male so that he could continue his Soul journey and grow as a man facing intense emotions and an authoritarian approach to personal suffering. They told him that they would help him to choose the highest path again and reassured him that he was not insane or being judged, that they were supporting him every step of the way.

When Andrew left it was like the weight of the world had been lifted from his shoulders. Plenty of challenges still remained, but the strange experience he'd had in the prison cell was now explained and it resonated deeply with this amazing young man. He resumed his studies, he did his community service work, he and his father pulled together, had more readings, attended counselling and went to see his parole officer as required.

Sadly, as part of his sentence the court ruled that Andrew must also consult a psychiatrist and this psychiatrist prescribed lithium, which Andrew is obliged to take for the duration of the parole. He experiences side effects from this medication but the psychiatrist insists and he is required to take it. His criminal record is also affecting his career prospects because now, even with a university degree under his belt, the court will not show him any leniency and will not allow him to leave the state to study or work elsewhere.

Despite all these challenges and setbacks Andrew remains positive and can see a future for himself. He and his father continue to petition the court for greater leniency, flexibility and we hope, an overturning of his original conviction. Yes Andrew did run amok, he admitted as much, he is not seeking to pretend that those things don't matter, he is seeking some compassion from a system that is supposed to deliver justice. There aren't many among us who would be able to cope with the sudden loss of a parent under such horrendous circumstances. Andrew now intends to use the rest of his life to prove that he is a better person than he was during that awful time in his life.

Uunderstanding that he is a star seed has also brought him a whole new appreciation of life and he now sees himself as the unique, sensitive, intuitive, wise and gifted Soul that he truly is.

If you believe that you might be a star seed what should you do?

My recommendation is to live your life as fully as all of us should in the knowledge that you are playing your part in this great cosmic story we call life. If you are suffering in any way I hope that the words in this chapter will help you to understand yourself more and have compassion for yourself. Yes, you probably feel very far from home at times, but while you are here on Earth this is your home and you chose this life and chose to be here. Who knows where the human race will be in generations to come and how valuable your experiences and connections may be.

If you are struggling to create and maintain balance, can't deal with the harshness of this physical reality or feel very disconnected from others then ask your Angels and Spirit Guides for help. They can communicate with your former civilisation on your behalf to inform them that you are finding certain aspects of Earthly life difficult. Your former civilisation can then adjust the connection they have with you so that you can feel more balanced and enjoy more harmonious circumstances. I don't know how they do this, the best analogy they have given me is that its like tuning you into a gentler frequency or rewriting your software. If you have a reading with me then this finetuning or rewriting usually happens during the session, but you are more than welcome to request this on your own behalf using your Angels and Guides as the go-betweens.

RECOMMENDED FURTHER READING:

Journey of Souls by Michael Newton
Destiny of Souls by Michael Newton
Pale Blue Dot by Carl Sagan
The Starseed Transmissions by Ken Carey
The Return of the Bird Tribes by Ken Carey

About the author

ABOUT THE AUTHOR

BelindaGrace grew up in Sydney and spent 25 years travelling around Australia and the world doing readings, and presenting courses and workshops. During this time she wrote five books and created three beautiful sets of oracle cards.

Now retired, she lives in the Northern Rivers of New South Wales, Australia, with her partner. She enjoys gardening, hiking, reading, studying French and Spanish, staying fit and of course checking in regularly with her Angels and Spirit Guides.

Ever passionate about helping people discover their hidden gifts and sense of life purpose, BelindaGrace continues to share this with you through this book, encouraging you to trust in your own inner wisdom and affirm every day that you are enough.

Acknowledgements

In writing a book there are always so many people to thank because their support, encouragement and belief are so invaluable. It is absolutely true that I could not have written this book without the presence of all the wonderful people in my life.

So it is here that I would like to offer heartfelt thanks to all my wonderful family and friends who have always and forever encouraged me, supported me and given me their feedback. Thank you for everything!

I would also like to thank Rockpool Publishing for helping me to realise my dream of becoming a published author and of keeping that dream alive so I could take my work around the world.

And of course, my Spirit Guides and Angels who have helped and guided me in ways that are too numerous to describe.

My heartfelt gratitude goes out to you all.

BelindaGrace

BelindaGrace